Keith Skipper's
Bumper Book
of Norfolk Squit

Keith Skipper's

BUMPER BOOK OF NORFOLK SQUIT

High Jinks, Hilarity & Hot Air
from Norfolk's Favourite Raconteur

HALSGROVE

Originally published by Halsgrove, 2006
Reprinted 2007

British Library Cataloguing-in-Publication Data
A CIP record for this title is available from the British Library

ISBN 978 1 84114 565 5

HALSGROVE
Halsgrove House
Ryelands Farm Industrial Estate
Bagley Green, Wellington,
Somerset TA21 9PZ
Tel: 01823 653777
Fax: 01823 216796
email: sales@halsgrove.com
website: www.halsgrove.com

Printed in Great Britain by CPI Antony Rowe Ltd., Chippenham, Wiltshire

Contents

Prologue

A Norfolk labourer did a hauling job. He was told he wouldn't get paid unless he put in a proper statement of account. He wrote out the following bill:

'Three cums and three goes at five bob a went = 15 bob.'

Acknowledgements

As the more observant reader will note, I am beside myself with glee at this opportunity to thank all who have helped me along the Norfolk squit trail. A perilous journey at times, when innocence and naivety set me up for harsh treatment as a country lad, it continues to attract native and newcomer alike as the only proper path to true Norfolk enlightenment.

I'm thankful now for early lessons from rural masters whose verbal dexterity and vivid imaginations added real colour to village life – and often earned them an extra pint of mild down the local, particularly from those at the sharp end of their natural talents.

I salute the generosity of thousands of readers and listeners who kept me gloriously supplied with squit rations during my years as a journalist and broadcaster on home soil. In many cases, their reward is a little corner in this volume dedicated to our distinctive sense of humour. Thanks also to countless enthusiasts ready to share little gems on my long-running entertainment rounds. 'I're got one fer yew!' has been the prelude to so many appreciative chuckles and a safe place in my squit notebook.

Of course, even squit has to be cooked properly before it's suitable to be set in front of folk in such big dollops. My wife, Diane – who has been forced to put up with my old squit for far too long – saved her kindest smile and keenest appetite for this mirthful menu as she turned all my raw ingredients into an impressive spread. Halsgrove publisher Simon Butler ordered the dish in the first place... so that ort ter larn him a lessun!

Pictorial support has come from many quarters but I extend special thanks to Alan Howard, Ron Shaw and the late Cliff Temple, whose generous friendship I valued for several years. Current Norfolk notables jumped at the invitation to take a ride on the Norfolk squit wagon while a host of old friends on the local entertainment circuit chipped in with favourite yarns. This may well be the biggest collection so far in the history of squit. But there's bound to be more to come. Long may it reign as Norfolk's unique contribution to the world of true culture.

Keith Skipper
Cromer, 2006

Weaned On Squit

Welcome to the wonderful world of Norfolk squit! It's the county's most precious commodity in the fight to stay true to the 'dew diffrunt' mantra, a tasty part of the natives' staple diet and highly recommended for newcomers with an appetite for integration. It can break down suspicions and barriers, especially in a village pub where the dialect is still on tap.

What is squit? So easy to savour, so hard to define. In simple terms, it's nonsense, light-hearted foolery. 'He talk a load o' ole squit!' is usually accompanied by a half-admiring smile and friendly nod towards the exponent. 'Dunt yew talk such squit!' may sound like an admonition but it is invariably handed out with a grin. Even those who dismiss it as rubbish, inconsequential chat to fill the time, will accept it carries an entertaining edge with the power to be puckish without being nasty.

I was soon knee-deep in squit as a lad raised in a mid-Norfolk village in those economically austere years after the Second World War. Perhaps a sense of humour came with the rusks and dried milk to a small cottage where 10 children (five girls and five boys) grew up in a climate of homely bewilderment.

Where on earth did those babies keep coming from? Was the Tilley lamp attracting them? Would the midwife appear every time the kettle boiled? These and other leading questions were later condensed into one of my favourite summaries for the emergence of large families... 'Mother was deaf. Dad asked if she wanted a cup of tea, or what ...' A neat fusion of Norfolk squit and important socio-cultural matters.

HEDGEROW SEAT – a Norfolk son of the soil tucks into his "fourses" and finds food for thought in the natural world around him.

Of course, membership of such a big brood – I came somewhere near the middle – meant some of the ragging could be barbed and highly personalised. But I like to think that helped prepare me for serious challenges ahead – grammar school adventures, work in the media, marriage, parenthood, losing my hair, failing a series of driving tests and suffering long-term technological dyslexia.

I can reel off a whole series of droll lines inspired by a crowded household, many of them recycled today by folk reared in homes with the luxuries of electricity, hot and cold running water and indoor toilets:

'There were so many nappies drying in the kitchen we had a rainbow in the front room.'

'We knocked a hole in the wall so we could dip our bread in next door's gravy.'

'Mother's dumplings were as big as footballs. You didn't know whether to eat 'em or kick 'em. And after you'd eaten 'em, you wished you'd kicked 'em!'

'Mrs Jones next door invented the Norfolk spin dryer – a hula hoop with pegs.'

'Mum couldn't afford Andrews' Liver Salts, so she used to put us on the pot and tell ghost stories. '

'We were very poor. When I was six, they bought me a hat so I could look out of the window.'

'My brother was so ugly Mum used to pull the pram rather than push it.'

Delightful social pointers to our country life when a tin bath in front of the fire was commonplace, and a visit to the little house at the bottom of the garden an expedition full of menace after dark.

Despite blatant shortcomings as a toiler next to the soil – 'next to useless' was the most flattering label I wore – I did help out on farms where my father and older brothers worked. Wise men of the fields soon put me to the squit sword, especially at harvest time when any weakness in the teamwork ethos became all too obvious.

Gert: "I go on hollerday ter fergit evrathing...."

Florrie: "Yis – an' when I open my suitcase I find I hev!"

Again, I can recite memorable lines from the farmyard script, most of them directed towards me with a mixture of pity and sarcasm. I coat these in broad dialect to do justice to the sharpness behind them:

'Go'an fetch a pail o' dry water.'

'Bring yar hoe, we're a gorn muckspreddin'.'

'That wire nettin' on the huh keep rain orff the hins.'

'How long's a short bit o'string?'

'Go'an git me a left-handed hammer.'

'If yew sniff them dandelions, yew'll wee the bed.'

'Dew yew want a' odd job, boy? Go 'an milk the bull – thass a' odd job.'

Squit among the haystacks. Take it in the right spirit or run the risk of suffering uncluttered abuse. I never fully graduated to the Agricultural Academy of Squit, but I collected enough O-levels to sustain me in the school classroom when the going got tough. Trouble was, some teachers, usually those without any experi-

A little bit o' Squit

Many years ago a horse cabby meeting the last train at Norwich saw an old lady come out of the station, look up at the stormy skies and pull her coat over her head.

"Hi, missus," he called. "Yew'll git yar behind wet."

"Dunt care 'bowt that," she replied. "Thass 80 year old. The hat's new."

A little bit o' Squit

Ethel was surprised to receive a visit from her younger sister who had moved away from Norfolk many years before.

"Dew yew know," exclaimed Ethel, "if that hent ha' bin yew, I wunt ha' known who that wuz!"

A little bit o' Squit

A Norfolk farmer supplied two new ploughs to his pair of ploughmen.

One took possession of one of the implements, saying to his colleague:

"I'll tearke this one – an' yew kin hev which one yew like."

ence of Norfolk's strange little traits, tended to confuse squit with disruptive tactics. One such overseer of my educational journey invited me to leave the grammar school lesson until I could be sensible. I departed with the suggestion I'd probably be back in 20 years' time. All I'd done was claim Chaucer got hold of the Pardoner's Tale when he saw it dangling at the back of his trousers.

Squit rescued me from several potentially nasty scrapes in the playground and on train journeys to and from school in Swaffham. I couldn't fight my way out of a fertiliser bag, but I could land a telling blow or two on the funnybone. There can be few more disarming experiences than being confronted by a scrawny Norfolk lad pretending to be oblivious to all dangers and threats and daring you to spoil his punchline after a deliberate build-up in front of an expectant crowd.

My years working on local newspapers and the local wireless, a span of over three decades, and a freelance career as writer, broadcaster and entertainer since 1995, leave me convinced that squit can continue to be a source of high amusement and cause for deep affection well into a new millennium. That belief is based on much more than simple sentiment or a cussed Norfolk streak designed to laugh at overwhelming odds.

It may be diluted to some extent by continuing waves of newcomers to the county. No doubt it will be ridiculed by those who care nothing for such parochial riches. However, it is too valuable, too vibrant, too resilient to be swept away on a tide of bland all-purpose alterations largely imposed on a place determined to maintain a mind and character of its own.

I have garnered hundreds of Norfolk yarns and anecdotes and examples of anything else that rings the squit bell. They are gathered in this book to show why that humour is so special and, in many cases, so different. Rural wit and laughter, the very essence of squit, stem from times when country folk had to provide their own fun or go without. Rough-and-ready verbal treatment could be meted out

Gert: "That Hector's a right ole pain-in-the-neck."

Florrie: "Thass funny – I hev a much lower opinyun o' him!"

with repetition and embellishment adding to the potency, not least when the target for this risible mixture came into view. Lesser mortals might construe this as spiteful, even downright cruel, but those 'in the know' accepted it as par for the comedy course.

Country writer Clarence Henry Warren, born in Kent in 1895, wrote: 'It is one of the most attractive features of country humour that it never quite loses its freshness. It may be passed on from generation to generation but it remains a coin whose mintage is never dulled with use. The same may be said of country expressions which are not necessarily humorous at all – metaphors and likewise and old phrases which, once coined, have never gone out of currency.'

He recalled a couple of his village shopkeeper father's sayings: 'It doesn't take long to do a five-minute job'. And to anybody out and about unusually early in the morning: 'You must have got up before you went anywhere.'

Old Mr Warren would have admired a couple of favourites from my childhood scene: 'That allus pick a wet day ter rain' and 'That dew git late earlier' when the clocks were altered.

There's also real satisfaction in stories where the underdog bites back, the downtrodden gets up out of the nettles, the simpleton rounds on the clever dick, the blunt object of ridicule suddenly finding a bright new pin to prick the balloon of pomposity. You'll find plenty of such examples in these pages, along with devastating put-downs reserved for less-than-gracious 'furriners' and a masterly use of understatement that adorns countless Norfolk stories.

This volume is a glowing testament to the enduring strength of Norfolk squit at a time when dull uniformity seeks to smother such precious items. Leading Norfolk personalities have readily accepted my invitation to offer their take on squit. I turn affectionately to past masters in print and on stage to underline its dynamic appeal over the years. I salute those still ploughing their fertile furrows today.

Perhaps my first tingle of true Norfolk excitement came with my father's advice not to fall under the spell of an endearing rural personality who called regularly at our cottage to spin yarns, wheedle jars of home-made jam out of the pantry and drink endless cups of tea. How did father put it as our visitor chuckled down the path, checking his pocket watch and waving goodbye without looking back?.... 'Dunt yew paggarter orl his squit, boy' carries so much more of a lyrical ring than 'Now, don't pay any regard to all his stuff and nonsense, my son'.

Dad knew he was on a loser in any language. That old country character became my role model as he kept the squit ball rolling throughout the 1950s.

After all, you have to worship someone who responds to the simple inquiry of 'where are you going?' with a shake of the head and a deadpan 'I ent gorn nowhere – I'm jest a'cummin' back.'

Past Masters

Norfolk squit's Hall of Fame parade is led by a buck-toothed postman, a garage proprietor and a multi-talented schoolmaster. Allan Smethurst, Sidney Grapes and Dick Bagnall-Oakeley immediately lend their gentle yet pungent songs and stories to any discussion about that special brand of humour doing the Norfolk rounds – and occasionally making an impact further afield.

ALLAN SMETHURST (1927–2000)

The Singing Postman sampled national fame when his first-class delivery, 'Hev Yew Gotta Loight, Boy?', set him on an unlikely pop pedestal in 1965. He even outsold the Beatles for a spell, at least in East Anglia, and that song still strikes a telling chord in Norfolk and beyond.

He worried that he might be remembered just for that number. In fact, his writing flair sprang from deeper wells than any desire or ability to perform on stage, and other winsome, wistful and witty compositions deserve to be shared as little slices of social history wrapped in the endearing delights of the Norfolk dialect. They are deceptively simple but crammed with potent images of a Norfolk life fast disappearing even as he wrote and sang about it.

Allan Smethurst's round as a celebrity in a postman's uniform all but ended in 1970 after a few brief years in the spotlight. He spent much of the rest of his life as a virtual recluse in a Salvation Army hostel in Grimsby. He had found it very difficult to cope with the pressures of stardom and his bill-topping summer season on Great Yarmouth's Golden Mile at the Windmill Theatre was cut short by illness brought on by stage fright and excessive drinking.

For all his obvious frailties, there's a timeless charm about his work, exemplified here by cheeky lyrics in his ditty 'Thass a Lot 'o Squit' and a delightful monologue he composed after the Great Train Robbery of 1963.

Gert: "The bank hev sent my cheque back."
Florrie: "Oh, thass good. What are yew gorn ter buy wi' it this time?"

THASS A LOT O' SQUIT

Twas on a Monday night when I wuz on m' bike
Pedallin' orl the way back home
As' a copper on the beat, he stopped me in the street
He asked me where I meant myself to roam.
Then he say ter me 'You hent a loight, I see'
I said I hed it when I came away
He give me such a look, scribbled in his book,
'Thass a lot o' squit' he say.

M' wife was at the door, mobbin' orl the more,
She say 'Now where the dickens hev yew bin?'
Then she start ter shout: 'I know you're bin about
Ter lead your little double life o' sin.'
I said I met a blonde, down along the prom.
She took me home ter pass the time o'day.
M' wife begin ter cry, she look me in the eye.
'Thass a lot o' squit' she say.

Well a long time ago when I wuz still at school,
The teacher used ter make a fool o' me
He used to bet the staff, jist ter get a laugh,
That noffin' I could dew wuz fit ter see.
Well he give me work ter dew an' when he read it through
He found I hed the answers orl okay.
Well he brook the pencil lead, then he turned a huey red,
'Thass a lot o' squit' he say.

Well ever since the day the army went away,
We're never hed the guns along the shore,
They used ter shoot the shells from Weybourne down ter Wells,
An' they never hit a dicky orl the war.
In 1939 the siren start ter whine,
An' they practised like the darvil for their pay.
Then a Heinkel came around, shot the target down,
'Thass a lot o' squit', they say.

Gert: "Did Gloria marry that painter an' decorator, then?"
Florrie: "Yis – she wuz overcome wi' emulshun!"

THE GREAT TRAIN ROBBERY

So old Charlie, he say to me, he say, they're still on about that big train robbery you know. Yis, I say, and tha's a lot a squit. So he say, how do yer mean tha's a lot of squit? Well, I say, all that money wass vallalas for a start. So, he say, how do yer mean that wass vallalas, won't worth narthin'? Well, I say, they wass goin' to burn it, I say, thay wass goin' to take it to one of these here incinerators and they wass goin' to burn it. So, he say, wass that gotta do with it?

Course tha's just like old Charlie, he ask yer a question. Yer tell 'im and he say wass that gotta do with it. Well, I say, tha's gotta lot a do with it. I say, if yer had suffun what yer considered valable, I say, yer won't burn it. Yer won't hull it on the fire. No tha' I won't, he say. Well no more would I, I say. Well, he say, vallalas or no, he say, they got the hul pleese force out arter it. Oh! I say, wass the idea a that? Well, he say, Thay want all that money back agin of course. What, I say, arter they wass gorn' ter burn it? Yis, he say. Well, I say tha's a rumin state of affairs, first they wass goin' to burn it, they were agoin despose if it, and now they want all that back? Of course, he say. Well, I say, if they really want tha' money back, I say I know how a git it back. Oh, he say, so yer think yerself a rear lot clevra than what they are. Well, I say, I'm clevver enough. Well, he say, how do yer propose to git all this here money back? Well, I say, let the robbers keep the money. Well, he say, how's tha' goin' git the money back if yer let em keep it? Well, I say, if yer let 'em keep it, the first thin' they'll do, they'll go to a bank, open a bankin' account, and tha's 'ow they'll git tha' money back. Oh, he say, they won't do that.

Well, I say, that strikes me as thou' they don't know whether they want tha' money back or no, I say. Well, he say, yer can't give two and a 'alf million pound away like that. Well, I say, they int got it to give away, so 'ow can they give it away? Well, he say, yer don't understand heconomics, he say. Well, I say, you don't call that' heconomical, burning two and 'alf million pound, I say, tha' int being heconomical. No, he say, tha' int what I mean, he say. He say, you hav' to have heconomics do you git inflation. Oh, I say, I didn't know we're talking about Bicycle tyres. No, he say, that int the kind of inflation I mean, he say. He say, yer can't do things like that he say. Yer har'a have gold, he say, that's the gold that covers it. He say, if yer int got the gold to cover this here money, he say, that's vallalas.

Well, I say, yer silly old fool, tha's what I say in the first place, and yer laugh. Oh... tha's different, he say, 'course tha's another one of Charlie's favourite saying tha's different, mind you, old Charlie, he say, do there caught some of 'em. Yis, I say, do yer know what ther' got. 30 odd years. Blast, he say, tha'll take em a ling time do that. Yis, I say, but some of 'em hav' escaped already. Yis, he say, tha' din't take them long to do tha'.

Gert: "He' yew noticed sum people ent like uther people?"
Florrie: "Yis – thass cors they're diffrunt."

SIDNEY GRAPES (1888 – 1958)

Sidney Grapes was a rustic comedian, garage owner and man of letters who lived all his life in the Broadland village of Potter Heigham.

He had made his mark as the archetypal Norfolk teller of tales at local concerts and dinners well before he dropped his first lines to the *Eastern Daily Press* in January, 1946, the start of an exercise destined to reach a much wider audience. The Boy John Letters were written in dialect but never swamped by it. The country cast list soon became household names – Boy John, Granfar, Aunt Agatha and the cantankerous Oul' Mrs W—.

Many readers, myself included when I discovered them in the early 1950s, used to cheat a bit and go straight to the 'P.S.' first for Aunt Agatha's latest example of homespun philosophy. Favourites are still exchanged regularly whenever Norfolk people meet and want to break the ice.

On stage, Sidney wore an old 'chummy' hat – a soft felt hat with a narrow brim – a smock and a 'ropper' round his neck. But those tempted to dismiss him as just another country bumpkin soon discovered he wasn't such a fool as he might have looked. He would get the audience laughing at him half way through a yarn and then up would go the admonishing finger – "Now, hold yew hard, tergether!" – and he would proceed to the cream of the joke in which the rustic triumphed and had the audience laughing with him.

Sidney also had several musical party pieces, some of them involving his dressing up as an old washerwoman ready to wring as much squit as possible out of the lines.

The Boy John Letters, with Aunt Agatha's wonderful postscripts, retain genuine charm and value because they are wholly unpretentious, gently amusing and admirably self-effacing. Here's my favourite epistle and some of Aunt Agatha's timeless sayings:

GRANFAR PUTS HIS FOOT IN IT

Deer Sar – Plearse dornt yow mob me acos I hearnt rit yow leartly, tha's acos I're bin moderate for tha best part o' sum time. I ha' bin at wark orf an on since Xmas. I heter hev tha Doctor. He gan me some narsty medicen. I believe they think, yow know, that tha nastier that tearst, tha more good that'll dew yer. He's given me injections now, so I get better sooner.

Granfar he ha' bin a keeping fit, only he ha' hed cramp, in bed. But he ha' cured that, I'll tell yow how. He say, 'When you teark yar shews orf afore you go to bed, stan 'em side by side, only mock em stan one shoe one way, an one tha tother, heel an toe tergether.'

He say, 'Agin, if you want to hev some good luck for tha day, when yow put yar shews on a' tha' mornen, put tha' left shew on furst, then you'll be orlrite fer tha' day.

Well, thank goodness, my Aunt ha' finished a spring cleanen. My hart that jorb upset a home, an as Granfar say, that dornt look no different when tha's done. My Aunt Agatha think that dew, but I know, an Granfar, he know, our home allus look clean, an tidy.

Oh, Granfar an Mrs. W- hed one set-tew. Mrs. W- wuss a helpen my Aunt Agatha ter spring clean. Just as Mrs. W- wuss a tearken a pail o' whitewarsh trew our rume, tew tha' scullery, tha Wicar called. Mrs. W- shoved tha pail o' whitewarsh on tha' stairs, an shut tha stairs door right quick.

Well, that would a bin orlrite, only Granfar, he'd laid in a bit leart that mornen. He wuss a cumen downstairs backwards, acos he's a gitten on, an blowed if he dint plump his hinder foot right inter that pail of whitewarsh.

Bor, he hallered. He sed a bad word, tha Wicar nearly heard him. I dussent say what tha bad ward wuss, but thet hed suffen ter do with a breeze o' wind.

Aunt Agatha she soon delt wi' tha situaweartion. She say to Mrs. W- 'You go an git on a white warshen tha scullery, an shut tha door. Granfar, tarn yow round an set down, dornt yow walk upstairs yit, dew you'll whitewarsh tha' whole stair carpet.

Well she warshed his foot, an he went up an put some more trowsers on, but my Aunt kep them tew apart fer tha rest o' tha day.

Well after tha spring cleanen my Aunt Agatha took Mrs. W- up ter Norridge, an they went ter tha posh new shop wuss just opened. Poor Mrs. W- had a calamity there. That wuss on them moven stairs. They wore a gorn up ter tha' next floor. She follered Aunt Agatha, but harf way up she got tha wind up, she cum a scrappen orf down agin, a knocken people about wot wore a gorne up. She dropped har shoppen bag, har oranges an onions wore a rollen downstairs, an yit they kep a gorne up agin.

At larst she got down agin. Har umberalar wot she stuck tew, had opened out. Some fellar what stood there sed, 'What'd yow cum down by parashute Missus?'

Well tha' starf wore werry good ter har, an they helped har to git har goods ter-garther. She got orl har onions orlrite, but she lorst three oranges (yer see there wuss a lot o' kids a gorne up and down a them stairs). O course Mrs. W- wuss upset, she told Aunt Agatha she thought a drop o' short would settle har narves, but Aunt Agatha took har ter hev a cup o' tea and she wuss soon orlrite agin.

Aunt Agatha told us orl about it when she got home, an dint Granfar larf!

Well, fare yer well, tergethar. – Yours obediently,

P.S.- Aunt Agatha, she say, 'It's far better for us to like what we have, than to have what we like.'

THE BOY JOHN
14 April 1956.

Gert: "Is yar family big on Christmas traditions?"

Florrie: "No – we jist dew searme ole things year arter year."

Aunt Agatha, She Say....

Aunt Agatha, she say, the only ordinary people in our villages are them what think they arn't.

Granfar, he say, salt is what make tearters tearste nasty if yew dunt put it in.

Aunt Agatha, she say, many a woman hev lorst a good sweetheart by a'marryin' on him.

Aunt Agatha, she say, thass no good a'puttin' yar foot down if yew hent got a leg ter stand on.

Aunt Agatha, she say, she's a very wise woman what say nothin' at the right time.

Aunt Agatha, she say, all husbands are alike, only they hev diffrunt fearces so yew kin tell 'em apart.

Aunt Agatha, she say, never hit a man when he's down – he might git up agin.

Aunt Agatha, she say, reality is when yew leave datty dishes in the sink – and them beggars are still there when yew git hoom.

Aunt Agatha, she say, if people think yew're a fewl, keep yer mouth shut, then they wunt know.

Aunt Agatha, she say, if yew want ter keep friends wi' the people in yar village, keep orf the parish council.

Aunt Agatha, she say, we're all sent her ter help the others. Granfar say, well, what the hell are the other beggars sent for?

Aunt Agatha, she say, yew carn't keep trubble from cummin', but yew dunt hev ter give it a chair ter sit on.

Gert: "How cum yer're gorn ter Millie's weddin' when yew hent bin invited?"

Florrie: "Well, I hent bein told ter stay away neither!"

A little bit o' Squit

Several years ago a young mechanic was called to a Norfolk farm at harvest time to mend the binder. It was an intricate job in sweltering conditions.

The farmer eventually turned to the mechanic and asked: "Do you drink?"

"Yis, that I dew" came the expectant reply.

"Good," said the farmer, "That should help keep the price of barley up."

Aunt Agatha, she say, thass good ter chearnje yer mind now an' agin - that help ter keep it clean.

Aunt Agatha, she say, the churchyards are full of people the world couldn't dew withowt.

Aunt Agatha, she say, a thrippeny bit ent so good as sixpence, thow that go to church more often.

Aunt Agatha, she say, that dunt matter what happens, there's allus sumwun knew that would.

Aunt Agatha, she say, I dunt like ter repeat gossip - but what else kin you dew with it?

Aunt Agatha, she say, then ent how long we live, thass what good we do while we're alive what count.

Aunt Agatha, she say, that ent what you look at, thass what you see when you do look.

Aunt Agatha, she say, Mrs W- is all a'worryin' about suffin. She's one o'them what worry because she hent got nothin' to worry about.

Aunt Agatha, she say, there's only one thing wuss than bein' torked about. Thass not bein' torked about.

Aunt Agatha, she say, allus tearke a pride in yarself. If yow are poor, dornt look poor.

Gert: "Are yew wun o' Mabel's oldest friends?"
Florrie: "Yis... she carnt git enny new'uns!"

Aunt Agatha, she say, poverty ent no disgrace, but that can be werry inconvenient.

Aunt Agatha, she say, she's werry glad she wunt born afore tea wus invented.

Aunt Agatha, she say, a man can be a fule an' not know it – but not if he's married.

Aunt Agatha, she say, marriage is a fine institution – for them what like institutions.

Aunt Agatha, she say, yow can mearke many a false step by standin still.

Aunt Agatha, she say, widows aren't the only ones who have *late* husbands.

Aunt Agatha, she say, that ent what gals know nowadays what bother the parents...
thass how they found out.

Aunt Agatha, she say, how nice that is to do noffin, and then rest arterwards.

Aunt Agatha, she say, yow can allus tell a Norfolk man, but yow can't tell him much.

Aunt Agatha, she say, thass a pity we can't live in the past – that would be so much cheaper.

Aunt Agatha, she say, helpful people are allus the most hopeful.

Aunt Agatha, she say, the cost of living is allus about the same – all you've got.

Aunt Agatha, she say, a man who can't smile shouldn't keep a shop.

Granfar, he say, if wimmun know so much, how cum they arsk so many ruddy questions?

A little bit o' Squit

Policeman: "What are you doing lying there in the gutter? Were you knocked over?"

Billy: "No, ole partner, I'm OK. I jist found this here parkin' space so I're sent the missus ter buy a car."

A little bit o' Squit

Two ancient fishermen stood on Cromer Pier sizing up the North Sea.

"Thass the most water I hev ever seen," said one.

"Yew hent seen noffin' yet," replied the other. "Thass jist the top of it."

DICK BAGNALL-OAKELEY (1908–1974)

A truly gifted all-rounder, Dick Bagnall-Oakeley spent his early years on the coast at Hemsby, where his father was vicar. He was educated at Gresham's in Holt, and read geography at Clare College, Cambridge. When he was 25 Dick was asked to 'hold the fort for a fortnight' as a geography teacher at Gresham's. He stayed for the rest of his teaching career.

Dick's skills were abundant and varied and he represented the county at hockey, athletics and rifle shooting. He made himself an authority on migrant birds in North Norfolk and was an expert on capturing all wildlife and plant life on film. His informative yet humorous talks both on local television programmes and at lectures throughout the region made him a well-known figure.

Often he would break into the Norfolk dialect which he loved and at which he was an acknowledged expert. He feared it was disappearing as an older generation died and vital parts of their vocabulary were lost.

Dick collapsed and died at the wheel of his car in April, 1974, while driving to Inverness, where he was to have given a lecture on ornithology. In a tribute, Logie Bruce Lockheart, his headmaster at Gresham's, described Dick as 'one of the last true all-rounders, an outstanding, if mildly eccentric, example of a species of Briton approaching extinction. His joie de vivre spilled over so that everyone else felt better for it.'

Dick warned: 'When you read Norfolk tales, remember that they are tales about a highly observant, subtle and recondite people. Therefore, always think twice before you laugh at a Norfolk tale – the laugh might be on you!'

Here are my favourites from the Bagnall-Oakeley collection:

HAIR-RAISING TRIP

Early in the coarse-fishing season I went down to the Sportsman' Arms staithe on Ormesby Broad and there I met old Dan Smith. Old Dan was a well known local character, always to be found by the waterside, basking in the busy life of the staithe and controlling the letting of the boats. Today he was standing self-consciously by the bus stop, smartly dressed up in this Sunday best.

'Where are you orf to t'day, Dan,' I said, 'all dressed up in yar best Sunday

go-ter-meetin' clothes?' (You'll observe that I always use my native Norfolk speech when addressing a fellow Norfolkman).

'I'm a garn ter th' horspital,' he replied. 'The ole doctor darn't like the look o'me.'

'How are you a-gorn to git there?' I enquired.

'On the half arter two-time bus.' Dan observed.

There was still three-quarters of an hour before the bus arrived, so I took Dan into the pub, and there we met one or two other local friends, and spent a happy time over a drink and a chat. So happy in fact that we forgot to watch the clock, and when we next thought about it, the bus had gone.

Dan was 'right concerned' at missing his appointment at the hospital, but one of our friends in the pub offered to give him a lift into Yarmouth to get there in time. He was one of those motorists who always enjoy driving really fast, and soon old Dan, who was more accustomed to boats than to fast cars, was embarked on a hair-raising journey, cowering and cringing in fright while the car cut round corners as it dodged and weaved its speedy way down the narrow country lanes to Yarmouth.

As Dan was deposited outside the hospital with two minutes to spare, he expressed his gratitude for the ride thus: 'Well, thank yer werra much young man, but never no more, nor, never no more! I wouldn't ride back along o'you fer a thousand quid! There yar, bor, as we wuz a garn down Cairster causeway, there wuz telegraph poles a'garn past like gravestones in a cemetery. You musta bin gorn a hundred mile an hour. Do you allus drive as fast as that?'

'Oh yes,' came the driver's reply. 'I go a good deal faster when I'm by myself.'

'Cor blast' retorted Dan. 'I'm suffin glad I don't ride along o' you when you're by yerself!'

LANTERN MAN

During the notorious winter of 1963, I was driving home in the evening after giving a talk in Cambridge. The driving conditions were the most atrocious I have ever known. Ruts had been ploughed by traffic in the deep snow on the road, and then the snow had frozen. Gingerly I picked my way across slippery iron-hard bars, cracks, ruts, channels, and pot-holes.

Going through Brandon I heard the snorting and gasping of a sports car revving up in the below-freezing temperature. Soon the car came out behind me from an inn yard, overtook me, and sped off up the frozen road to Swaffham. Like the tortoise following the hare, my car continued to grind painfully through the packed snow. There was no other traffic on the road.

What happened next? You've guessed it. Some way further up the Brandon/Swaffham road, in the heart of the inhospitable Breckland, in the most cruel time of the year, I saw two red lights. As I inched my car nearer, I eventually

> **Gert:** "Yar hat's on the wrong way...."
> **Florrie:** "How dew yew know which way I'm a'gorn?"

realised in the darkness that not only were they the tail lights of a sports car, not only were they off the road, but the driver had hit one of the many iron-hard mounds on the uneven road at high speed, slewed off the road, and turned the car completely upside down in the ditch. There he hung, suspended upside down in his seat by a safety belt.

I had travelled the road many times before, but I had never previously noticed a small cottage among the trees at that particular stretch. Now however, out of it, with his shoulders bent against the wind and his lamp flickering, shuffled an old man. His comment on the situation was another example of that breathtaking use of understatement which I have found so often in Norfolk. It stamped him too, immediately, as a Norfolk man.

'What, are yer in a little bit o' a muddle?'

ON THE SHORE

In that same winter of 1963 I was making a film on the changes of habit imposed upon seabirds by prolonged exposure to hunger and severe cold. I chose a spot on the coast near Salthouse as the ideal view for a long background shot upon which the credits for the film could be superimposed. I arrived a little early on a bitter evening in February with the temperature reading eight degrees of frost, and I stood in the lee of a small cliff for the sun to sink to the right angle.

One other person went down to the cold, desolate stretch of coastline that evening. He was an old beachcomber, raggedly but warmly dressed, wheeling his bicycle with him, on the off chance that a plank might be there among the drift-wood washed up by the freezing tide.

For about twenty minutes I stood in such shelter as the cliff provided, but the sun still had not descended to the angle I wanted before the beachcomber had completed his tour and started to return. He passed me, still standing in eight degrees of frost, immobile in the same position as I had been in when he passed before. This time he spoke as he passed, and in the one word he uttered I heard all the plain speech, the avoidance of the play of 'polite' conversation, the laconic brevity and the shrewd humour that I have come to know and love in Norfolk people. Not a shabby, anonymous beachcomber, he summed himself up in an expression echoing all the ironic humour and the unanswerable understatement of a true Norfolk character.

'Sweatin'?'

Gert: "Children are a gret comfort in yar old age…"
Florrie: "Yis – an' they help yew ter git there a lot quicker anorl!"

Laughter Lines

In my roles as broadcaster and writer for well over 40 years, I have received countless letters blessed with a healthy Norfolk tang to share with all those who appreciate true culture.
Here's a selection of my favourites, largely reproduced just as they were written to underline the fact that there are no strict rules when it comes to employing the local vernacular. It's more a matter of personal taste and interpretation – and in some cases the full flavour comes with a reading out loud.

PROBATE SAGA

Freddie and Jimmie, two elderly bachelor brothers who lived in a village in darkest Norfolk, had a maiden aunt Ada Thirkettle who died aged 94 leaving them her entire estate. However, after 12 months nothing had been heard about the legacy.

One morning, Jimmie suddenly resolved to take Freddie to Norwich in the dickey cart and find out if anything had transpired. On their arrival at the solicitor's office, Jimmie said: "Right, Freddie, bor, sit yew here an' mind the dickey an' cart an' I'll go in an' see the solicitor."

He entered the office and explained to the solicitor about his aunt's passing the year before and there being no result concerning her will. The solicitor disappeared into a nearby office and returned with a file which he began to peruse.

After a couple of minutes he turned to Jimmie and said: "Well, it appears that a bill of probate has been taken out, but I'm afraid there has been a rupture in the proceedings at Somerset House and until we can get the assignees together to prove, I'm afraid you won't get any money."

"Right, marster". Jimmie returned to the street where he was greeted with "Woss he say, bor?" from Freddie who was sitting in the cart.

Jimmie confessed: "Well, thass like this. Old Billa Probert he' fell down in that old summer house an' ruptured hisself, an' until they git his arse an' knees tergether, we aren't a'goin' ter git no money!"

Richard Shepheard - Melton Constable

BUS PASS

This true story comes from the late 1940s on the Fakenham to King's Lynn run. The bus concerned was a Bedford WD coach with straight cut gears, or crash gearboxes as they were known. The driver, well liked by all his passengers, was not very good at double declutching and so all his gear changes were noisy to say the least. He missed the trip one day, and a new and most capable driver was at the wheel.

A regular passenger, a lady who suffered from flatulence, boarded as usual at

A little bit o' Squit

Billy went for a job on a building site. The foreman asked: "Can you make tea?"

Billy said: "Yis."

"And can you drive a fork-lift truck?"

"Why, how big is yar teapot?"

Burnham Deepdale. Before the bus had travelled very far she realised that her normal habit of relieving the pressure during gear changes was going to be difficult.

She hoped that when they turned from the main road at Holme for Ringstead and Sedgeford over the hills he would make some noise. No such luck. On to Fring, Shernborne and Sandringham. Still no noise, nowhere to take advantage. Through to Babingley and up to Castle Rising where the main road ran before the bypass was built.

By this time the dear lady was feeling desperate … But she knew the regular driver always made a terrible noise when they rounded the corner at the Black Horse. She prepared herself. When the driver's hand moved to the lever for that change to second gear – she let go. The wind roared through the bus. All conversation ceased.

To hide her embarrassment the woman said in a loud voice: "Driver, have you a timetable?"

"No, madam, I hent" he replied with no hint of a smirk. "But the next ole tree I pass, I'll grab yew a handful o' leaves."

Gerald Teeling- Sedgeford

TASTY NAME

When my family first arrived in the village of Felthorpe just over 70 years ago, my father, Albert Rumsby, who was gamekeeper for Mr Desmond Buxton, thought he ought to get to know the villagers as soon as possible for obvious reasons.

At the first shoot my dad organised for his new boss, he was told by a neighbour that "Old Hanner Meart" was a good beater. My mother was intrigued as to who could possibly own such a name. Inquiries were made and it turned out to be a Mr Stannard who worked for a local farmer.

One day his wife took his sandwiches into the field, as women did in those days. He pulled them apart, only to discover he had cheese in them. In a rage, he yelled at her: "Dint ya hanner meart?" ("Didn't you have any meat?")

Sadly, most of those old times have passed away – and much of the Norfolk dialect went with them.

Betty Barrett - Felthorpe

> **Gert:** "I hear Bill an' Ethel wuz happily married for tew year…."
> **Florrie:** "Yis – 1967 an' 1974!"

VET'S PROGRESS

Many years ago, when I was a small boy at North Creake, I recall a veterinary surgeon from Burnham Market named Frederick Gooderson, known to farmer and farm labourer alike as Freddie. Mr Gooderson, although a first-class veterinary, also had a liking for a drop of Scotch and was more often nearer drunk than sober.

Freddie travelled from farm to farm in a horse and cart. On one such occasion he was on his way from Wells to North Creake. When passing the Golden Gates, one of the entrances to Holkham Park, he cut the corner rather fine which resulted in the over-turn of the cart and Freddie hitting the road. He was knocked unconscious.

A gamekeeper was first on the scene and was rendering first aid when Freddie the vet came round and said: "Where am I? Where am I?". The gamekeeper replied: "You're at the Golden Gates, sir."
Freddie smiled and said: "Thank God for that. I never thought I should make it!"

Ted Beales - Docking

HARD RATIONS

The farmer, one of the board of governors for the workhouse, was on a visit when he spied one of his old farm labourers.

"Hello, George" he said. "I dint know yew wuz in here. How dew yew like it?"

"That ent so bad" said George, "but the grub ent up to a lot."

"I'm sorry to hear that. Woss wrong with it?" asked the farmer.

Feeling in his inside pocket, George took out a pea and held it out to the farmer. "Yew try an' crack that wi' yar teeth" said George. The farmer did so and said: "Yew're right, George, thass suffin hard."

"Yis," replied George. "An' that hev alriddy bin through me twice!"

Chris Basey - Acle

CUTTING HUMOUR

A friend who had been in the RAF at Lakenheath during the Second World War was in Brandon. He decided to have a haircut. He said to the barber: "It's over 40 years since I last sat in this chair."

"Yes," came the response. "That was my father. He did used to give good value for money."

Cliff Flodgell - Mildenhall

> **Gert**: "That gal Elsie git them good looks from har father."
>
> **Florrie**: "Oh, woss he a plastic surgeon?"

ON THE BAWL
Memories of the Rev Ronnie Cooling, Vicar of Martham 1968–1975.

Ronnie Cooling was a bachelor, born in Eire, who before he was ordained into the Church of England was an artificer in a Lowestoft shipyard. His skill was to be seen in the wonderful working steam railway models which he created from scratch.

Top Squit Ten

TOP TUNES

Here's a list of the most-whistled tunes in Norfolk villages as rendered by errand boys, paraffin delivery men, midwives on bicycles and road workers seeking a new spot to place traffic lights.

1. Walsingham Matilda
2. Pennies From Hevingham
3. Concrete and Cley
4. A Thurton Smile
5. Move Over, Larling
6. Anmer Down My Walking Cane
7. Bye, Bye Blackborough
8. I Wonder Who's Gissing Her Now
9. Blow the Wind Southery
10. It's a Long Way to Little Snoring.

Ronnie was a diminutive figure, probably less than five feet tall. He told me the story of how a rather swarthy elderly lady appeared at his door. She wouldn't enter the vicarage, but just came out with: "Vicar, I want you to christen my grandson next Sunday."

Rather taken aback by this approach, Ronnie politely inquired as to who she was and where she lived in the parish. She told him that she was one of the "travellers" whose caravans were just off the road on the outskirts of Martham. "All right," said Ronnie, "bring the lad with his mother and father to the church on Sunday afternoon."

The grandmother duly turned up with all the "travellers" and their many children and Ronnie started the service. One thing bothered him – the child to be baptised was about three years old and almost half the size of the vicar.

Amid all the noise from the children, Ronnie came to the actual baptism.

Because of the size of the child, he decided to sit the boy on the rather large marble font and baptise him there. Immediately the boy began to bawl his head off.

After a few minutes of this, the old lady piped up: "Vicar, can I say something?"

"Yes," said Ronnie, resignedly. "Well, if you get that boy's arse off that cold slab, he'll stop bawlin'!"

As Ronnie said: "I did, and he did." And he continued the rest of the service with all the decorum he could muster, trying very hard not to burst out laughing at a rather unusual intrusion into a religious service.

Rev Ivan Lilley - Attleborough

Gert: "I will say that gal Ethel dew speak har mind...."
Florrie: "Well, that must limit har conversation a fair bit."

TOP OF CLASS

Many years ago there were reports of low standards in Norfolk schools. The authorities were so alarmed they sent a special inspector to investigate.

Arriving at a village school, he introduced himself, explained his mission to the head-mistress and asked if he might question some of the pupils. He started with a boy he considered none too bright.

"Now, I walk down a road 200yards wide and half a mile high. How old am I?"

The boy replied without hesitation: "Forty-tew, sar."

This happened to be the inspector's correct age. Asked how he arrived at the answer the boy said with a smile: "Well, I're got a bruther at hoom woss 21 – an' he's only harf a fewl!"

George Jessup - Watton

TOTTING UP

Walter was getting on more than just a bit, but in spite of this he was still most virile and, indeed, very proud of it.

One night as he sat by the fire with Tilly, his devoted and grateful spouse, he declared: "Gel, Tiller, I'd like yew ter keep a book what kept a record o'when we got tergether."

"Orlright, boy Walter, if thass what yew want then thass what I'll dew."

The months went on and one night Walter remembered his request. "Tiller, did yew keep that there book what I asked yew ter keep?"

"Yis, that I did, boy Walter."

"Well, less ha' a look at it."

The journal produced, Walter proceeded to read in a serious manner. Over a long period it worked out Monday once, Wednesday twice, Friday once, Saturday once.....

All of a sudden it went up a gear. Sunday three times, Monday, Tuesday, Wednesday, Thursday twice each and a final flourish of another three on the Friday.

"Cor, blarst!" said Walter. "I dint think I wuz that good."

"Yew wunt" said Tilly. "That wuz the week yew went away an' stayed wi' yar brother out at Wroxham."

Tony Palmer - Caister

Gert: "They reckun ole Cyril dew hev hidden talents...."
Florrie: "Well, the search go on!"

IN THE WARS

This story is a bit unsavoury, but it shows how we lived in a Norfolk village, Middleton, near King's Lynn, in the early 1940s. We had no flush toilet, just a bucket which had to be emptied fairly often as we were a family of five.

A little bit o' Squit

Billy came home from work to find his young wife in tears.

"Oh, William," she sobbed, "the first meat pie I ever baked for you, and the cat got it."

Billy consoled her. "Dunt yew fret, my bewty. I'll get yew another cat ter-morrer."

It was not desirable to have too much urine in the bucket so my father, my brother and myself when in need of a pee used to use one of the shrubberies which surrounded the house. It may seem a filthy habit nowadays, but we never gave it a second thought. Female members of the family, of course, were allowed to use the toilet for all purposes.

There was a chamber pot under each bed which my mother used to empty every day into a drain just outside the house. One night on going up to bed she realised she had overlooked this chore. As it was teeming with rain she went to the window and tipped the contents of the pot into the yard below.

At the same time, my father, wanting his last pee before going to bed, decided it was raining too much for a walk to the shrubbery. So he walked to a drain in the corner of the yard which happened to be directly under the bedroom window. As you may have guessed, the two events coincided and father was showered with the contents of the chamber pot.

I was told by my mother that went he eventually dared to open his mouth his language was something she did not wish to ever hear again.

They both laughed about it later – but only one was laughing on the night.

Lionel Jackson - Ely

CONFESSION TIME

My wife and I went to a slide show one evening about three or four years ago in a local "hut". After a while a couple of ladies came and sat themselves down next to us in the row. They were both into the autumn of their lives.

I soon noticed how they started to nudge each other and giggle a bit. The object of their amusement appeared to be two equally aged gentlemen sitting directly in front of them. Eventually one of the ladies tapped one of the men on the shoulder and said: "Tom? It is Tom, isn't it? And Harry?"

The men looked round and smiled but didn't say anything. The woman then said: "it's a long time ago and I don't expect you remember, but when we were teenagers

Gert: "They dew say munny ent evrathing....."
Florrie: "No – but thass a long way ahid o' whatever cum next!"

you and your friend biked home with me and my friend. It was one night after we met in the Regal at Beccles. Do you remember?"

Tom laughed and said: "Yes, I remember biking home with a couple of gals. That was a bit of a laugh, cos we were just looking for a bit of fun that night. Mary and Jane, wasn't it?"

At this the two women burst into laughter. Tears rolled down their cheeks as one of them said: "We have a confession to make. Our names were not Mary and Jane, we just said that."

Tom replied: "Well, we didn't tell you our real names either. I'm not Tom and he's not Harry!"

As you can well imagine, the four of them didn't take much notice of the rest of the evening's proceedings.

Ray Edwards - Brampton, nr Beccles

IT'S OBVIOUS!

At a reception class in a Norfolk village school the teacher was using a word-and-picture-matching game. One by one the children had to come out and match up word and picture, but were told not to help each other.

One small lad was very slow and stood looking at the row of words for two or three minutes. His little friend stood it as long as he could, dancing from one foot to the other in his impatience to help his playmate. At last he could stand it no longer. He exploded with: "Goo on, Graham, thass a hollerin' at yer!"

Bert Miller - Horsham St Faith

CANON CORNERED

I see my ole mate Billa Phillipo t'other day. He's youngest son o' ole Charlie Phillipo, what used ter be biggest ole poacher fer miles around.

When young Billa wuz born, ole Canon Watson went ter see his mother. (Parsons had time fer wisitin' then an' could afford ter pay a curate tew preach his sarmons on Sundays)

"Now, Missus Phillipo," say the Canon, "may I ask how large your family has now become?"

"This here's my tharteenth, Raverend," she say.

"Well, Missus Phillipo," say ole Canon, "I would like you to give a message to your husband for me, if you would be so kind. Just tell him that I think the time has come for him to grease his gun and stand it in the corner."

When Charlie cum hoom his missus say: "I hed the ole parson ter see me terday."

"Oo 'ar" say Charlie, "an' what did he want?"

"Well," she say, "He axed arter the little 'un an' then he say as how I wuz ter gi' yew a message. He say he think the time hev cum fer yew tew grease yar gun an' stand it in the corner."

"What did yew say?" say Charlie.

"Well," say his missus, "I looked th'ole fella straight in the eye an' I told him – thass like this here, Raverend. My husband hev had the shootin' over my estate fer a gret number o' years now, an' so long as there's a hare on it he shall continue to do so."

John Gray - Pulham Market

*GOING UP!
Horsepower harvest
at Burnham Overy
with the elevator going
full pelt, and the boy waiting to lead the horse back
into action after the load has
been emptied.*

HORSE POWER

As a schoolboy I worked in the harvest fields calling "Hold-gee!" which meant the chap on top of the wagon load had to hold tight and the horse had to "gee" (go).

A farmer was telling me about his first tractor. He sold his two horses and came home with a new machine. This was in the days when farmers had bikes.

He came up to the straw stack and couldn't remember how to stop. He shouted: "Whoaa! Whoaa!"

The tractor went into the stack and he couldn't get to the handle to restart it. So he had to ask for his horses back to pull it out.

John Tye - Swanton Morley

DOUBLE SETBACK

Here's a story my father used to tell.

A motorist was lost in the countryside when he saw a man and boy hoeing sugar beet. He called the boy over.

"Could you tell me the way to White House Farm, lad?"

"No, that I carn't, sar" replied the boy.

So the motorist continued along a very narrow road that curved in a horseshoe shape around the big field. Just as he got to the far side, he glanced across and saw the boy waving frantically.

The driver reversed with great difficulty to where the boy was eagerly awaiting him.

"I hev asked ole Billa over there if he know where White House Farm be" said the boy. "An', he say he dunt know neither!"

Yvonne Fuller - Aldeby

Gert: "That Elsie dew hev wun o'them hour-glass figures....."
Florrie: "Yis – but thass gittin' a lot later than she think!"

30

A little bit o' Squit

Billy: "I hent got nun."
  Teacher: "You must not say that, Billy. You must say: 'I have none.
My mother has none. My sister has none.' Now, what do we say?"
  Billy: "Nobody hent got nun."

WANDERING BILLY

As a young girl at the start of the first world war, my mother was on tour with her parents' repertory company when they played Norfolk. As her elder brothers had been called up, Mabel, my mum, was often obliged to play male roles and sometimes even double.

On this particular night she was playing the Good Fairy and Billy the village idiot in a pantomime. Now, Billy was always played in the dialect of the area they were in. Mabel was pretty good at the Cornish accent and around and up to Sussex. She could do a fair Cockney and an excellent Yorkshire – but Norfolk eluded her no matter how hard she tried.

On the night, the principal girl asked: "You are in trouble again, aren't you, Billy? What have you been up to this time?"

Billy shuffled his feet and was supposed to say: "I only peppered the cat's eyes to make him sneeze."

Up to now Mabel's accent had been wandering all over the country and in desperation her line came out as: "I ony peppered the cat's arse to mak 'im snaze!" You can imagine how this went down with a hearty Norfolk audience. They roared with laughter and applauded Billy madly at every entrance after that.

Peggy Ferguson - Thetford

THAT'S BETTER!

About 30 years ago when one of my nieces was an infant teacher, members of her class were re-enacting the tales of Uncle Remus.

One of the small boys said in a dull monotone: "Here come Brer Rabbit." He was told to use more expression, more surprise in his voice.

So his next effort began: "CORD, BUGGER ME! IF THAT ENT OLE BRER RABBIT!"

Kenneth Adcock - Stoke Holy Cross

Gert: "My photos dunt dew me justice."
Florrie: " Yew dunt want justice – yew want mercy!"

FOLLOW THE ROAD

While pursuing enquiries in the depths of West Norfolk, in an area of flat, open land-scape, my police colleagues and I found we were out of our depth. We were lost.

On a long and straight barren road, bordered by fields stretching into infinity, we spied a rustic gentleman of ancient vintage pushing a cycle of equal antiquity. I found that country working men more often pushed their cycles than rode them.

We stopped and asked the way to a certain village. The countryman stopped pushing his cycle and leant on the handlebars to consider the question. He was wearing a floppy hat pulled down over his ears, a raincoat tied in the middle with string and baggy trousers tied at the ankles, probably string again.

"Well," he said after much thought and without looking at us. "Thass like this, boy. Yew go as the road go."

With that he shuffled off without a backward glance. We did. He was right.

Maurice Morson - Norfolk Police

THERE'S A LIMIT

Several years ago during a darts match at Hempton Bell we were discussing the proposed new licensing laws and arguing that it would be a good thing if there was no such thing as "Time, gentlemen, please!" This really was discussed at length.

Tom sat in the corner quietly taking it all in. When all had finished he summed up very simply by saying: "Yew carnt only drink a gutful!"

The other incident came at the Royal Norfolk Show. One chap said to the other: "How'd yew git on wi' that ole sow yew bort larst year?"

"Wuh," he replied, "that wunt no good. The fust time that pigged that dint he'-nun, an' the second time that hed two – an' they et each uther!"

John Tuck - Pudding Norton

Gert: "They dew reckun Rupert wuz born wi' a silver
spoon in his mouth."

Florrie: "Oh, p'raps thass why he hent stirred since!"

NORFOLK FIRSTS

The County is famous for many things but there are a great number of feats and fascinating facts for which Norfolk can claim to be 'First' and of which the general population is entirely ignorant. To set the record straight I have chosen to publish for the first time a selection of just a few 'Norfolk Firsts' in order that the county may in future claim them for its own.

1

Norfolk's first travelling family folklore troupe were the Bloomer Brothers of Brockdish, pictured here on their initial outing of 1903. They launched a new season of what they call "futility rights" in their distinctive costumes with a traditional two-step dance and a chorus of: "Plant your taters when you will, they won't come up before April." They were in constant demand to visit allotments in the Diss area as the horticultural scene came alive. Even hardened cynics were hard pushed to explain why county produce shows were dominated for over a decade by Shimpling shallots, Roydon radishes, Burston beetroot and Lopham leeks. The brothers also performed regularly at garden fetes, arts festivals fashion shows, rural crafts displays, real ale galas and private functions demanding a traditional flavour. They disbanded in 1922 after a late frost destroyed an entire pea crop at Palgrave.

2

Norfolk's first woman archery champion was Bertha 'Bullseye' Fletcher of Bowthorpe. She carried off the crown in 1898 when her home parish three miles west of Norwich had a population of only 58. Unable to attract local sponsorship after retaining the county title three years running, she moved to Shotesham and won backing from village bookmaker Laddie Brooks. Their joint slogan 'Our Tips Are Always On Target' became the best-known in Norfolk sporting society during the opening years of the twentieth century. They married in 1910, Bertha's friends providing an archway of Cupid's arrows for the bride and her beau, and Laddie's colleagues took bets on how many more times his new wife would win the county championship. In fact, Bertha added another string to her bow a few months later when she became coach to Norfolk's William Tell Club at Appleton, hitherto an all-male preserve, and promptly retired from serious competition.

3

Norfolk's first successful ventriloquist was Bob Martin of Rougham, who made his mark with an unusual act featuring two terrier dogs. Bob's little canine chums, Fetch and Carrie, spoke impeccable English while their owner simply barked in response to questions from them. This novel approach was destined to hit trouble when Bob developed a bad sore throat during his routine at Weasenham St Peter Variety Club Awards evening in September, 1922. The dogs whispered hoarsely that the other member of their act had to go into quarantine, and patrons were offered their money back or a free ticket to an exemption dog show at Cockley Cley. Bob retired from the entertainment scene in 1929 after catching mild distemper. Fetch and Carrie went into kennels at Mutford and organised elocution lessons for other animals hoping to get into show business.

4

Norfolk's first competitors in the modern Olympic Games were Maurice and Millicent Raleigh, from Mileham. They took part in the 5000 metres mixed doubles cycle race at the newly-built White City Stadium in the London Games of 1908. Millicent's slow puncture on the opening lap of their first-round meeting with couples from Italy, France and Essex did not prevent them from reaching the next stage, but hopes of a Norfolk flavour in the final were dashed by a freak collision between Maurice and the starter. As the pistol fired, and competitors rose from putting on their cycle clips, Maurice's boater slipped over his eyes. He lost his bearings and rode straight at the official perched on a wooden box at the side of the track. "Raleigh cleared of taking illegal substances – but must take a new proficiency test" was one of the big stories of the 1908 Olympics. The couple founded Mid-Norfolk Family Cycling Holidays later that year and are pictured with daughter Isabelle in a promotional tour of Tittleshall.

5

Norfolk's first woman vet, Jane Harriott, opened her dispensary for sick animals at Horsey in 1922, transferring to bigger premises at Oxnead two years later. She attracted national interest for her novel way of treating some younger patients, talking to them in sharp tones rather than applying any orthodox medical cures. "Crisp counselling saves time and money" she told The Goatkeeper's Weekly after being accused of kidology, gruff manners and upsetting Capricorn readers. Miss Harriott's unusual methods also included smearing mint sauce on lambs' tails, placing apples in noisy piglet's mouths and sending stressed turkeys for weekend breaks in Great Witchingham. She retired to Catfield to write her memoirs and confessed to not liking animals in the slightest. All Creatures Grate and Smell, with a foreword by Ralf Horris, is now out of print.

Gert: "At least that gal Doris dunt go in fer gossip....."

Florrie: "Oh, so thass why she hent got no friends ter speak of."

A little bit o' Squit

Horry had a sign outside his home. It read: "Beware of the canary."

A newcomer to the village asked: "Why should anyone be scared of a canary?"

Horry replied: "Cors this one whistle fer the dawg."

Top Squit Ten

DRAMATIC BEST

Here is a list of favourite dramatic productions in rehearsal among Norfolk's cultural set. Curtain up on the top ten plays for the village hall stage:

1. Weeting for Godot
2. Look Back in Anmer
3. Fransham Without Tears
4. Scole for Scandal
5. Heydon Fever
6. Chicken Soup With Barney
7. The Trowsetrap
8. Much Ado About Rougham
9. The Lady's Not For Burnham
10. All's Well That Bawdeswell

6
Norfolk's first hornpipe dancing expert was Lionel "Longshore" Leggett, a fisherman from Wells. He diversified after holing his boat, Wee Willie Winkle, off Brancaster and losing the entire catch in 1922. As well as organising hornpipe dancing classes on Thursday afternoons, with music provided by close friend Eric "Ebbtide" Sands on his squeezebox, Lionel made a colourful mark on the local modelling scene. Specialising in oilskins, and always appearing with trademark clay pipe and sou'wester, he became a popular figure on the catwalks of Stiffkey, Cockthorpe and Burnham Deepdale. He opened Lionel's Boateak in Wells in 1931, but this bold business venture was sunk when his net profit failed to reach double figures. A successful recipe book, 101 Things To Do With Samphire, and a social club for retired twitchers, The Old Crow's Nest, provided for a comfortable retirement at Dunsteppin on a new estate in Quarles.

7
Norfolk's first outdoor poetry-reading festival for "Genteel Young Ladies of a Literary Disposition" was held on Gorleston Cosies in May, 1931. Sadly, after only eight lines of Christina Rossetti's Goblin Market, read by Miss Primrose Gore-Booth of Upper Sheringham, the event was curtailed by high winds. It was staged the following year in a curing shed at Winterton, but the festival rapidly declined after Miss Gore-Booth eloped to Southwold with a wet-fish merchant.

8

Norfolk's first home-grown pantomime star was Mabel Mason of Sedgeford. She made a promising mark with several local entertainment troupes, including Ringstead Revellers, Fring Frolickers and Docking Delectables, before joining Heacham Headliners in 1905. Billed as "The Mawther with the Mostest", Mabel took the title role in the society's first production of Cinderella, and drew rave notices with her sultry looks, pleasing voice and energetic broomstick dance. This saw "a dynamo in a liberty bodice defy gravity, reduce Prince Charming to a frazzle and turn the Ugly Sisters into a lather of lamentations".

Such success sparked a dramatic tug-of-war when Hunstanton Humdingers tried to lure her away from their artistic colleagues along the coast – but Mabel settled the matter by returning to her home village to form Sedgeford Sorcerers. Their revues, Sufferin' Suffragettes and Lloyd George Knows My Father, won Bafta awards (Brancaster Academy for Tactile Arts).

Mabel had a short spell as choreographer for Stanhoe Stompers in 1925 before retiring from the stage and opening a teashop in Kettlestone.

9

Norfolk's first theme park was opened at Spooner Row, near Wymondham, in 1908 by the Bill & Co Leisure Group. Designed with newly-weds in mind, The Love Nest featured a network of rustic bridges over exotic vegetation and pools in which couples could see their reflections.

Honeymooners James and Amanda Godwick are pictured on the Bridge of Thighs, a favourite posing spot towards the end of the trail. The park flourished until 1913 when a rival concern, Call It a Day, aimed at couples considering separation or divorce, was launched at Ditchingham. This went into liquidation on the outbreak of the First World War. The Love Nest, soon overgrown and neglected, became a nature reserve notable for an abundance of nightingales. In 1958 James and Amanda Godwick celebrated their golden wedding with an emotional return to Spooner Row, camping as close to their honeymoon location as possible. "This area is very good for arthritis," said James. "We both got it within three hours of arriving."

Gert: "Wunt that be luverly ter hev evrathing?"

Florrie: "No – yew wunt know where ter put it!"

10

Norfolk's first professional removals service was launched by Jabez "Flit" Flockhart at East Raynham in 1897. His next-door neighbour asked for help after deciding to switch to West Raynham because of lower business rates, and Jabez provided a cart pulled by Dilly the donkey. Other bookings soon followed for trips for Colkirk, Toftrees and Helhoughton, and Jabez had to purchase a bigger cart and an extra donkey. He built up a fleet of six vehicles and eight animals and transferred the growing concern to Wellingham in 1908. Sadly, the loss of a chiffonier, coal scuttle and fairground organ on a journey to Thursford undermined confidence in his services, and he sold out to Wells Cargo Express Removals on the eve of the first world war. Jabez tried to invent the charabanc boot sale in the 1920s, but the Norfolk public remained unmoved by such far-seeing business acumen.

11

Norfolk's first junior sea angling champion was seven-year-old Hector "Salty" Saunders of Sea Palling. He burst on the competitive scene in dramatic fashion in 1934 by lifting the Captain Hook Cup from an inaugural entry of 31 on Cromer Pier. Wearing what was to become his trademark outfit of matching green and brown sou'wester and oilskin top, young Hector took top prize with a 66lb catch of cod, bass, mackerel, mullet and crabs. Asked for the secret of initial success by a local reporter, he cited a mixture of beginner's luck, a coypu-based bait and "my grandad's secret tips" on how to fix the pin at the end of his home-made willow rod. Many other trophies followed, but his debut haul remained the highlight of Hector's long career. He was Norfolk's small-boat champion in the 1950s and opened his own angling accessories store at Tacolneston before returning to the coast to write instruction manuals. Those still in print include Cast Your Bait to the Winds, Make a Rod for Your Own Beck and A Shore Weigh to Tip the Scales.

Gert: "Are yew a'goin' ter that Adam an' Eve ball?"
Florrie: "Yis – leaves orff at midnyte!"

12

Norfolk's first national champion milkmaid was Deirdre Muffett (pictured here) of Pulham St Mary. She took over a herd of 50 cattle at the Nicecream Parlour in the village in 1922, and milked them all by hand twice a day. Her remarkable productivity led to success in a competition run by the Dairy Dispatch magazine. She was crowned Top Gallon Gal in 1924, a title she did not yield in five years. Deirdre retired to write handbooks for a new generation of dairy workers, Beyond the Pail and Any Udder Business went into several editions, while her memoirs, Pasteurise Before You See It, were serialised in the Milk Marketing Board's monthly newsletter, Cream Tease.

13

Norfolk's first outdoor dentist's surgery was opened wide at Pulham Market in 1921.

Early trials to perfect the latest equipment were held at the bottom of the garden behind new bungalows at the north end of the village. Volunteers were paid a half-crown to test the "tooth theory". Senior partner D K Nash transferred the business to Gasthorpe and then on to Castle Acre, where he was appointed the county's first Royal Dentist. Junior partner Phil Ling emigrated and built the world's biggest false teeth factory in Massachusetts.

14

Norfolk's first pet-sitting service was set up by Norah Boon of Saddlebow, near King's Lynn, in 1936. She became a familiar figure in the area taking dogs for a spin in her bicycle basket, although efforts to provide similar treats for cats, mice, bantams and budgies proved less successful. Her reputation as a colourful carer reached a peak when she insisted on giving a Sandringham-based corgi a ride to Tilney St Lawrence in a snowstorm. Norah lost only one pet in her charge, a bloodhound from Marham which turned up on the Hardwick roundabout pawing a lift three weeks later. It is reckoned that but for the outbreak of war she would have made a small fortune out of her burgeoning "bark-and-ride" service.

15

Norfolk's first official town crier was Gabriel Walter, who used the title "Premier Proclaimer" when he took up his duties at Harleston in the 1920s. In fact, he was also the county's first village caller, rousing farmworkers from their beds around 4am in his home parish of Yelverton before the first world war. As he suffered regularly from colds and sore throats in those days, Gabriel gave four short blasts on his horn beneath bedroom windows to indicate it was time to rise. He is pictured shortly before giving up all engagements in 1937, demonstrating how he had started his outstanding career of public service. A report in the Harleston Bugle struck a few amusing notes, although the writer clearly got carried away with all the musical imagery – "Captain Hornblower can no longer tame the high Cs... Gone with the wind, but the melody lingers on... Gabriel ready to spread his wings into retirement... Last shout before the civic blow-out."

16

Norfolk's first couple to plan to run away to Gretna Green were domestic servant Ethel Grimes and market gardener Percy Pointer in June, 1924. In fact, Percy's motorcycle broke down a few miles from their home village of Hoe, and they cancelled the elopement for a year, after a picnic on Gressenhall Green. An argument over cress sandwiches and a faulty piston raised doubts about their relationship – doubts to be erased by over half a century of happy travelling together. They celebrated their golden wedding at a motorcycle maintenance class at Swanton Morley when Percy described Ethel as "one in a pillion" and Ethel called Percy her "revved-up-Romeo". Friends and relations presented them with a new piston and a map of Scotland.

17

Norfolk's first outdoor wedding reception was held at Eaton Park in Norwich in 1903. The caterers, Big Portions of Pudding Norton, prepared 50,000 gallons of oxtail soup, 800 crans of fresh herring and 1450 barrels of home-made parsnip wine. The newlyweds, "Tip" Scales of Egmere and Belinda Rash of Baconsthorpe, later enjoyed a fish and chip supper with their 41 guests before leaving for a honeymoon at Burnham Overy.

Gifts to the happy couple included luncheon vouchers from colleagues at the slimming club they ran at Weybourne, Wishful Shrinking, and a book of health food recipes from the groom's friends at Brancaster. The bride carried self-raising flowers, courtesy of Dahlia Smith Bouquets of Dumpling Green, and helped with the washing-up after changing into her going-away clothes.

18
Norfolk's first nightclub door-men were drawn from Billy Ball's Barton Bendish Bouncers in 1927. Renowned for their fitness and teamwork, most notably in the breathtaking feat of all balancing on the back seat of a moving bicycle, they made their mark as peacemakers at a notorious Stoke Ferry speakeasy, The Bosky Mawkin, and the West Dereham 24-hour dancing emporium, Pally Glide. They fell out after their annual tour of pubs around Swaffham Market in 1932. Nine of them joined local gymnastic troupes while the others became male models for the off-the-peg clothing chain Anglican Combinations of Wimbotsham.

19
Norfolk's first full-time weather forecaster was Sam "Stifler" Snelling of Brancaster Staithe. After a lengthy career as a fisherman and boat repairer, he set up his own meteorological office in Howsomever Cottage at the north end of the village in 1924. Always dressed in oil-skins – "Jist in cearse that tann a bit rafty" – he relied entirely on old country lore and family tradition. Sam's stock rose dra-matically when he advised local farmers that barley should never be sown in spring until "the soil feel warm ter yer backside". He was consulted regularly by fete organisers, warning them to scan the night skies before setting up stalls: "When the stars begin ter huddle, the earth'll soon become a puddle." He also reminded all who called: "If there's ice in November ter bear a duck, there's noffin arter but slush an' muck". Through ignoring his own counsel – "Dunt sit on the grass in any month what hev an R innit" – he caught a chill in November, 1933 and died at 91 on a fresh but bright day later in the month. The inscription on this headstone reads: "Grief melts away like snow in May."

Top Squit Ten

REAL MEANINGS

A rash of groovy labels on everyday items continues to dominate our language. But salvation is nigh. Trendybabble must make way for propaspeak, sensible, old-fashioned Norfolk words and expressions. Here are some examples:

1. Worst-case scenario – suffin' bad
2. Postive feedback – wholly good
3. Let's run this up the flagpole and see who salutes – hent got a clue woss goin' on!
4. At the end of the day – shuttin-up time
5. Level playing field – hent bin built on...yit
6. At this moment in time – 'bowt now, I reckun
7. Can you run that past me again? – sorry, wunt listenin'
8. I hear what you say – dunt tork such squit!
9. I see where you're coming from – yew dunt fewl me!
10. When all is said and done – thass yer lot!

A little bit o' Squit

On a job application form beside the question regarding marital status, a Norfolk labourer wrote: "Nut speakin'".

A little bit o' Squit

The teacher was trying to point her Norfolk class towards good grammar. "You should never say 'I see him do it'," she told them. "Yis," piped up Charlie at the back. "Speshally if yew ent sure he dunnit."

Laitiers Flamande

20

Norfolk's first "a la carte" meals on wheels service brought hot soup and cold custard to elderly folk living in remote areas around Saham Toney in the late 1890s. Organisers Jabez and Martha Bistow used dogs to pull what they called their "wittles wagon". The service lasted three years before badly-rutted roads made it impossible to transport liquid food this way. Social services provided a coach and pair for final deliveries in 1899. The couple opened a tea room in Bodney with its famous slogan: "Thirst come, thirst served", and completed their catering days running a transport café in Didlington. A notice in the window read: "Don't stand outside and look miserable. Come inside and be fed up."

Gert: "Dew yew hev enny good ideas how ter keep my bills down?"

Florrie: "Yis, my ole bewty – use a paperweight!"

21

Norfolk's first model agency for children was opened at Harpley in 1906 by retired society hostess Hermione Hardcastle. At one time she had more than 100 "cutietots" on her books and many privileged Norfolk youngsters featured in leading publications of the day. A few, like Bonnie Barmer, pictured with her mentor, were snapped up by big fashion houses to boost sales of children's clothes. Bonnie appeared in one magazine so often it was suggested it might be renamed Harpley's Bazaar. Although the fashion industry was in its infancy, Hermione Hardcastle knew the value of an innocent smile and little stumble on the catwalk. She opened a second branch at Sculthorpe, but had become disillusioned with the business by the end of the Edwardian era in 1910. Greedy parents and crafty agents tried to dictate terms while youngsters demanded extra sweets and freedom to negotiate contracts for advertising new products. Hermione gave it all up – and became a non-executive director of a public relations firm in Flitcham.

22

Norfolk's first Young Farmer of the Year was Percival Petman, who collected the honour in 1909 when he was 11 and helping out regularly on his uncle's smallholding at Stockton. Percival cut his agricultural teeth scaring crows, singling sugar beet and chasing rats at threshing time – long before health and safety rules and regulations – and he could milk by hand a large herd of cows before he was nine. Hard work and a competitive edge brought many more plaudits, including the Horkey Highlow for completing an entire harvest on his own with a scythe at Wheatacre, and the Tricolator Trophy for mending a dozen wooden ploughs in under an hour at Brooke. After retiring from the land, he tried basket-making at Kirby Cane and mattress-stuffing at Bedingham before setting up a successful chimney-sweeping business at Broome.

23

Norfolk's first professional carol singers were the Marks Brothers of Halvergate. Graham, Charles, Harry and Zebedee all had demanding office jobs by day in Yarmouth, but enjoyed dressing up and entertaining after work. They formed the Quavering Quartet in 1899, based at Halvergate Hare and Hounds and it became traditional for them to present a concert of seasonal delights every Christmas. An argument over the number of free drinks to which they were entitled led to a switch to the other village pub, the Red Lion, in 1919...but that proved a short-lived stage for their talents. Regulars objected when the brothers insisted on miming Silent Night, and then changing words of well-known carols to suit their own style.

We Four Kings of Ormesby Are, O, Little Town of Burlingham, and In the Bleak Mid-Winterton, upset the purists. The quartet took to the streets, and are pictured performing outside the blacksmith's shop in the nearby parish of Freethorpe. A lucrative little local career ended at Wickhampton where they were set upon by dogs for serenading the village schoolmistress with The First Knowall.

24

Norfolk's first licensed private eye was Desmond Marlowe of Seething. Dandy Des, as he became known in the 1930s by virtue of natty garb and accessories, started serious investigating after losing his umbrella at a speakeasy in Beccles. He traced it to an isolated farmhouse near Topcroft – and it never left his grasp again while the Dandy Des Detective Agency flourished. Perhaps his finest hour was solving the case of the missing trellis at a Hempnall nursery when the culprit asked for 328 other fences to be taken into consideration. With his probing days over, Desmond took up the pen to write a series of successful novels set in the mean streets of Mundham, including Hello, My Bewty, the Little Doze, and The Quick Cheerio. He retired to sheltered housing in Kirstead, calling his apartment "Dun Sleuthin" at Shurelock Homes.

25

Norfolk's first travelling horticultural service, Rakes Progress, grew out of the enterprise of first world war veteran Digger Trench from Limpenhoe. His door-to-door venture, launched in 1919, blossomed into a county-wide operation with biggest branches at Barton Turf (laying lawns), Clippesby (hedge trimming) and Ditchingham (drainage of heavy soil). Digger met his wife, Charlene Dimmock of Spooner Row, during early days on his rounds. Our picture shows them discussing the best ways of forcing early rhubarb. They married at Little Cressingham in 1922, borrowing 10 shillings from Breckland Allotment Holders' Association to pay for the reception. When they retired to Hethersett in 1934, they admitted to having made a "considerable pile" out of clearing and cultivating all kinds of plots.

26

Norfolk's first star of silent films was Mollie Coddell, of Scratby, who landed a screen test after winning three seaside beauty competitions in the early 1920s. She became Miss Hemsby, Miss Caister and Miss California, her third title convincing famous film director Darryl Z Pepperpicker IV that she had the right credentials for a leading role in Yanks for the Memories. As Mollie did not have to speak in front of the camera, it was generally accepted she hailed from America. She went to Hollywood in 1929 as an established silent screen actress and made a mark in several talking pictures as an English rose with an appealing country accent. Mollie returned to Norfolk just after the second world war and appeared in many local stage productions, most notably Annie Get Your Gun and No, No Nanette with the Martham Mummers. She also enjoyed a summer season at Gorleston Pavilion, topping the bill in the revue Resorting To Laughs, before retiring to Filby and taking up bowls and flower arranging.

27

Norfolk's first successful pop group, The Bronickle Boys, set maidens' hearts a-fluttering just after the First World War. The chain-smoking gang, comprising Vic, Mick, Dick and Isaac, started entertaining as a close-harmony act on returning to their home village of Lessingham and soon became big favourites at local concerts. They topped the bill for a season at the Old Trunch Empire in 1924, when the programme also included fire-eater Billy St John Beard, The Stewkey Blues Band and female impersonator Walsingham Matilda. The Bronickle Boys won a recording contract with Black Shuck label a year later, and their first long-player, Songs to Clear Your Throat For, sold nearly 30 copies. It included memorable Norfolk-inspired numbers such as Narborough Fair, Ashill Grove, Etling Greensleeves and It's a Long Way

to Little Fransham. The group broke up at the height of their fame following an argument over the Eurovision Song Contest. Isaac went solo with his entry Blow the Wind Southery – he finished equal 14th with Norway – while his former colleagues founded The Tizzick Trio and enjoyed several years as cabaret performers in the smoke-filled nightclubs of Barton Turf. They disbanded after the coughing epidemic of 1937.

28

Norfolk's first rural counsellor, offering free advice and support to overworked agricultural labourers, was Chimbley Jinks of Calthorpe. Pictured here at an impromptu session in a farmyard at Erpingham in 1919, he claimed to have "a sustificate in high-larned squit" obtained from "a high skewl on a hill near Aylsham". Employers were reluctant to encourage him at first, but he won them over with his quiet, philosophical approach to glaring problems in the countryside. Indeed, several farmers sought counselling themselves after their men had attended one of Chimbley's outdoor surgeries, dubbed "mardling dews". His most famous contribution to easing rural strife came in the early 1920s when he persuaded Norfolk farmworkers on strike, and bosses reluctant to even talk about meeting their demands, to organise a "harmony horkey" on Hanworth Common. Peace broke out after 29 barrels of mild beer and a round of traditional harvest songs. Chimbley, a teetotaller and occasional Methodist lay preacher, was carried shoulder-high to Aldborough Green where he organised a similar event under the banner: "Dunt let stress caws a mess."

Gert: "I hear cantankrus ole Charlie's bin in horspital wi' his lege…"

Florrie: "Yis – an' he got Git Well Soon cards from all the nasses!"

29

Norfolk's first millennium dome for small family outings was created at Cockthorpe in 1921, thus defying the county's reputation for always being behind the times. Official opening of what was dubbed the "thrillennium vault" to avoid accusations of jumping the gun, was delayed for three weeks. It was discovered there was no doorway, while safety inspectors insisted on a rigorous no-smoking policy in the body zone. The firm behind the project, World-wide Wonders of Warham, went on to build slightly larger attractions at Langham, Stiffkey and Little Snoring. Our picture shows last-minute preparations at Cockthorpe by the multi-screen team of Hick Ling, Bess Ingham and Jean-Claude Pierre Debussy. Attendances slumped when an electronic playground was introduced behind the dome to take minds off the General Strike in 1926, and the building was put in a time capsule for safe keeping. Unfortunately, no-one kept a record of exactly where it was buried on Cley marshes.

30

Norfolk's first mountain rescue team, who became famous as the Sherpas of Shipdham, were members of the same family. Edward, Charles and Eliza Hillary showed early signs of being prepared to take risks to help others when they formed a little convoy for visits to the village shop. It stood on top of a steep incline and they would signal to locals below if any traffic was coming the other way. Holidays in undulating parts of Norfolk alerted them to dangers of climbing out of one's depth, so to speak, and they won considerable praise for going to the aid of an elderly couple stranded on the notorious north face of Beeston Bump, near Sheringham, in the summer of 1929. The intrepid trio completed their training at the Peak Fitness centre close by Acle Straight, and concentrated activities on the Runton Range, near Cromer, and Happisburgh Heights. In all, they rescued more than 500 tourists suffering from vertigo and delusive behaviour prompted by rumours that Norfolk was flat. They retired at the height of their fame to start a coypu farm in Switzerland.

A little bit o' Squit

Sign seen in a Yarmouth amusement arcade: "Don't thump the machine. Look for an attendant."

31

Norfolk's first official holiday guide, Hadrian Mule of Happisburgh, was appointed in 1906 when a charabanc was spotted heading for Overstrand. There had been no reports of bookings at any of the local apartments, and residents were anxious to avoid an influx of itinerant trippers. Hadrian's initial brief was to "be as awkward as it takes to make them feel less than welcome." Decked out in rustic garb, he feigned deafness, shook his stick angrily at anyone he didn't recognise or understand and said Poppyland was just the other side of Thetford. Strangely, his antics encouraged visitors rather than put them off and his reputation grew as a colourful harbinger of genuine Norfolk character and heritage. Hadrian capitalised on such notoriety by organising coastline walks "in the pawmarks of Black Shuck", ending with pub grub at a hostelry run by the Walcott Wallop Brewery. The Hound of the Basketmeals became a free house in 1929 and Hadrian Mule (aged 81 and three months) retired from the blossoming holiday trade the following year to become a lifeguard in a car-wash at Waxham.

32

Norfolk's first attempt to organise a home-grown lottery met with only partial success. A syndicate of former tax inspectors converted on old steamer, the OHMS Revenue, into a floating casino off California (near Scratby) in 1926. The Top Deck Draw was abandoned after a fortnight when the same six numbers emerged in successive weeks and the same six men shared a jackpot of three guineas, 211 crans of freshly-caught herring and a season ticket for Hemsby's Golden Furlong arcades. The syndicate made a fortune when they sold the vessel to Yarmouth Borough Council as an overflow area for large gatherings of travellers.

> **Gert:** " Is that ryte Walter cum from a werry poor family? "
> **Florrie:** " Yis – his parents got married jist fer the rice!"

Lancers—Last figure.

Arranged by A. E. Brown, V.P.B.A.T.D.
New Walk, Leicester

33

Norfolk's first ballroom dancing academy, Knockin' and Toppin', was opened in Beetley in 1911. Instructors Edith Steplightly and William Lummox provided "partners with poise, tuition with tact, music with melody and the best lemonade crystals this side of Guist." They specialised in local versions of popular dances such as Foxley Foxtrot, Pentney Polka, Tuttington Tango, Wayland Fling, Mundford Minuet, Gaywood Gordons, Paston Doblé, Garvestone Gavotte and Sloley Quickstep. The academy formation team, The Pollywiggles, reached the area final of a special competition featuring crinolines, cravats and buskins, but had to bend the knee to winners Wendling Warmints. Edith and William closed their establishment after a short-lived revival in the 1920s and took their talents to a holiday camp on the South Coast. Their memoirs, Partners in Time, were published by the Trouser Press in 1949 as they retired to the Last Waltz Rest Home in Swanton Novas.

34

Norfolk's first woman winner of the prestigious Loddon to Beighton New Car Rally was Michelle Shoemaker of Booton. She romped home ahead of a star-studded field in 1906, posing with Muttley, her "pit-stop terrier" for this picture in Combustion Capers, forerunner of the Pirelli Calendar. Michelle's trailblazing victory was due in no small measure to most of her rivals taking a wrong turning in Norton Subcourse while she made tracks for Reedham Ferry. A smooth crossing on her own left sufficient time to mend a puncture on Freethorpe Common, beat off footpads at Wickhampton and support a Suffragettes' bring-and-buy sale at Hassingham. She collected the coveted Iceni Trophy from rally organiser Monty Carleton Road – and promptly announced her retirement

from the sport to spend more time with her family and on her hobby of hat-making. "I think I have seen Norfolk roads at their best" she mused. Muttley barked agreement.

Gert: "Did yew notice that heavy fog larst night?"
Florrie: "No I dint – noffin wearke me up."

35

Norfolk's first high-speed courier service was launched by the "Macadam Mawthers" at Blo' Norton in 1936. Mona (driver), Deirdre (sidecar) and Amy (pusher-off and telephone sales) retired to the Isle of Man after selling the business to an ARP warden on the outbreak of war. They formed a concert party to entertain at the famous TT races and won many plaudits as "The Pillionaires".

Harvesting sugar beet the old-fashioned way in Norfolk, a back-breaking chore in the depth of winter.

Top Squit Ten

THERE'S NOENDONEM

There's a old Norfolk habit of running several words into each other. Here's an account of growing and harvesting sugar beet in the days before mechanisation.

1. Adrillenonem
2. Ahoenonemwiaoss
3. Achopenonemout
4. Asingleonem
5. Afeedenonem
6. Ahoenonemaginwiaoss
7. Amowldenonemup
8. Ahoenonemaginwiaoss
9. Apullenonem
10. Aknockantopenonem
and one for luck: Accountenonem

That wasn't the endonem as they had to be taken to the side of a road to wait for a permit to come through from the beet factory, loaded again onto the tumbril, taken two miles to the station and unloaded on to trucks.

Gert: "Hev I parked the car orryte?"
Florrie: " Well, thass only a short walk ter the pavement."

A TON OF FUN

It's mighty hard to ration squit. I thought it would be relatively easy to confine myself to
one hundred cherished yarns for this special harvest of humour. However, many old friends
who have been good to me over the years must accept a long-distance wave as the only
acknowledgement for now. Those privileged to be invited to an exclusive reception can show true
gratitude by hailing each story as a typically cussed pebble of native defiance dropped in the ocean
of standardisation.
All right, I freely admit some yarns have done, and are still doing, the rounds elsewhere and
earn inclusion simply through being given a local lick of paint. Yes, most of those colourfully
coated in dialect were created to be told rather than read. Several were inspired by a closely-knit
agricultural world long disappeared over the headlands. But they represent a deep and durable
affection for the past as well as getting to the heart of a continuing campaign to wage war against
insuperable odds.
Here's my ton of fun presented with pride in the old Norfolk saying that laughter
improves your face value.

DRY OBSERVATION

Two American servicemen failed to negotiate the A47 bend at Burlingham on the road to Yarmouth during
the last war.

They ended up in a pit alongside the road. They managed to crawl out but the car was left upside down
in the water.

As they surveyed the sad scene, the local blacksmith arrived. He observed dryly: "One good thing abowt
it – if yew wuz thinkin' o'dewin' a job on the bottom, now's your time, ole partners."

DOUBLE TROUBLE

The newly-married Norfolk farmworker went to a lot of trouble over the whitewashing of his cottage.

Asked about his thoroughness, he replied: "Well, the larst tew families what lived here hed twins. I'm jist
mearkin' sure there ent no infection."

HE LOOKED!

An agricultural worker went to a Norfolk farmer for a job. He was asked for a character reference from his
last employer.

"Well, marster, I did hev one, but I lorst it."

"You must be a fool losing it like that" said the farmer.

"Nut such a fewl as yew think" said the worker. "Yew see, ole bewty, I'd read it."

PLAYING WITH FIRE

A tramp on his way from Ipswich to Norwich came to the George and Dragon Inn. He decided to try his
luck.

His knock on the back door summoned the landlady who shouted: "Clear off, you lazy good-for-nothing
creature!" She slammed the door in his face.

As he turned towards the open road again, the tramp passed the open kitchen window.

He pushed his head through and asked: "Any chance of a word with George?"

A little bit o' Squit

Old Fred the marshman took aim at a lone duck overhead. "Jist yew watch this" he commanded a large band of onlookers.

He fired. The bird flew on.

"There yew are, my bewties," said Fred.

"Thass a miracle yew're a seein'... a dead duck still a'flyin'!"

BREATHLESS SPELL

The headmaster's study in a Norfolk school was up a flight of stairs. One morning there was a knock on the door. A stout woman entered, very much out of breath.

"Now, what can I do for you?" asked the headmaster.

His visitor puffed and panted. "I couldn't send my mawther Mary ter school terday."

"Well, why didn't you send me a note, then?"

"But I couldn't let mawther Mary come ter school terday."

"Yes, but surely a note would have sufficed."

"Blarst, yew dunt think I would ha' climbed orl these bloomin' steps, dew yer," said the breathless one, "if I could ha' spelt diarrhoea?"

SIMPLE MENU

An old Norfolk bachelor lived alone with his dog. When he retired he was persuaded to have meals-on-wheels.

Four years later, old Jimmy said to the delivery lady: "Yew wunt need ter call enny more, missus."

"Oh dear, is there something wrong?"

"Yis – the dawg is dead, and I like bread an' cheese m'self."

HAIR-RAISING NEWS

This story concerns a boy apprentice in a barber's shop at Bungay during the last war. A customer asked the barber if he'd heard the latest.

"What's that, then?"

"The Jarmans he' got Tobruk."

At home that evening the boy was so quiet his mother asked him: "Is suffin worryin' yew?"

"Yis, Mum. Them Jarmans he' got to Brooke – so they might well be here termorrer."

Gert: "What did Myrtle dew afore she wuz married?"

Florrie: "Ennything she wanted tew!"

Gert: I have harf a mind ter go inter polytics..."

Florrie: "Well, my ole bewty, thass orl yew need!"

TALKING SHOP

Back in the 1930s a shopkeeper in a remote Norfolk village kept a commercial traveller waiting.

The only assistant was a young girl who, standing on a stool to reach a tin of peas, dislodged some others. One crashed on to the commercial traveller's head.

Luckily he was wearing a hard black hat. This was knocked over his eyes.

To be so ill-used while waiting patiently for orders was bad enough. But the poor man's humiliation was complete as the shopkeeper snapped: "Hey, dew yew be more careful, Daphne – that might ha'bin a customer!"

PAYING HIM BACK

Old Nathan Nobbs, the village builder employing six local men, was a bit of a skinflint. He agreed to pay them for Christmas Day but said if they wanted Boxing Day off it would be without pay.

When he arrived at the yard on Boxing Day morning none of the men had turned up. But he found a large notice pinned to the gate. It read:

"Owing tew bizness bein' slack, Nathan Nobbs, builder of this parish, hev bin unable ter pay his men for thar Boxin' Day holiday. It is hoped that by next autumn trade will hev improved so he kin pay 'em for the two minnits' silence on Armistice Day."

SLOW BUSINESS

A Norfolk newspaper reporter was told of a village where there hadn't been a funeral for over 20 years. "They seemed to live there for ever!" he scribbled in his notebook and decided to investigate.

On reaching the village he was shocked to see a funeral procession about to enter the church. He turned to a bystander and exclaimed: "They told me nobody ever died in this parish. Here I am on my first visit, and what do I see but a funeral. Who is the unlucky parishioner and what did he die of?"

The ancient local stroked his chin and answered quietly: "Oh, that ent no parishioner. Thass the doctor. Jist died o' starvation."

VEGETABLE PLOT

Billy was in prison for something he didn't do. He didn't wear gloves. He knew all the prison mail was censored.

He got a letter from his wife asking about the family garden: "When dew I plant the spuds?"

He wrote back: "Dunt yew dig up our garden whatever yew dew. Thass where I buried all that money."

His wife wrote back a few days later: "Six policemen come to the house an' they dug up every square inch o' the back garden."

By return of post she got the answer: "Right – now yew kin plant the spuds."

Top Squit Ten

FETE ACCOMPLI

Try this list of fresh attractions to lure extra customers and boost takings at the local fete. It underlines the strength of creative urges, especially in villages where the fete remains the social centrepiece and locals savour annual reunions:

1. Bowling for the coypu (blindfolded)
2. Spot the country smell (newcomers only)
3. Bouncy castle for grandparents
4. Hurl a dumpling (removed from saucepan)
5. Skateboard race for parish councillors
6. Treasure hunt for nuclear waste
7. Dwile flonking in the dark (mixed pairs)
8. Estimate size of vicar's stipend
9. Guess the scarecrow's middle name
10. Weekenders and second-homers in the stocks.

Gert: "Hev that Mrs Harker got orl har own teeth? "
Florrie: "Yis – I wuz with har when she bort 'em."

POTATO RINGS

A Norfolk farmer asked one of his workers to go to the telephone box in the village and ring up the Potato Marketing Board.

About an hour later the farmer went to the phone box and found his man still inside. He asked if he had made the call.

"Cor, blarst, give a bloke a chance," came the reply. "I hev bin a'lookin' threw the Ts fer Taters... but I'm beggared if I kin find it ennywhere."

STANDING ORDER

Teacher said to Charlie's class: "Will all those who think they might be stupid stand up."

For a moment no-one stirred. Then Charlie got to his feet.

"Charlie" said the teacher, "do you think you are stupid?"

"Nut reely, Miss" he replied. "I jist dint like ter see yew standin' there by yarself."

KEEPING TRACK

Jack was strolling across the field when he saw Stan hoeing the sugar beet.

"What time dew yew knock orff?"

"Five o'clock."

"He' yew got a watch.?"

"No, I hent got a watch."

"So how dew yew know when thass time ter knock orff?"

"Well, yew see there's a railway line over there. A train go parst at ha'past five, so if I pack up harf an hour afore that git here, I know I'm abowt right."

IN THE WINGS

Some Norfolk children were playing Mums and Dads in the lane as the parson came by.

He smiled and then saw one small disconsolate boy sitting round the corner, well away from the rest.

The parson asked why he wasn't playing with the others.

"But I am, sar," said the little one.

"And what part would you be playing, then, my child?"

"Please sar, I'm a little ole bearby woss waitin' ter be born."

CLASS ROLE

It was time for the annual village school play and Ernie had been given a part. He was very excited and rushed home to tell his parents.

"Yew will come an' see it, wunt yer?"

"Cors we will" said Mum.

"What part hev yew got?" asked Dad.

"Oh, I play a man celebratin' his 25th wedding anniversary."

"Never mind, boy" said Dad. "Praps yew'll git a speakin' part next year."

A little bit o' Squit

A young lad went to stay with his grandparents on their Norfolk farm. The boy coaxed Grandad into letting him ride on the tractor during the ploughing.

Grandma asked what they'd been doing in the field. The boy replied: "Well I don't know whether we're taking the earth out or putting it back... but we're making it wider."

BEYOND THE PAIL

Wally Feeke and his honeycart inspired a load of cultural yarns in and around Litcham during the years when such carriages of convenience did regular rounds. The night-soil collection vehicle had several names – one with a bell was dubbed the humdinger – but the honeycart was a strong favourite in Norfolk

Wally never had to wait for service in Litcham's fish and chip shop – even when it was packed. The crowd parted like the Red Sea when Wally walked in. Every job has its perks.

American servicemen hijacked his chariot one night and charged up the Lexham Road at full gallop. They returned with more than a whiff of scandal. They had travelled at such a rate, the movements of the cart's contents forced up the lid. The hijackers were chastened and soaked.

The most popular yarn to surface down the honeycart trail is the tasty one about two chaps busy on their calls. It was warm going, so one took off his jacket and hung it on the back of the cart. A few minutes later he noticed it had fallen in. He tried to rescue it. His pal said: "That wunt be a lot o'cop arter that lot." Back came the reply: "I ent worried 'bowt the jacket, ole partner. I'm arter the sandwiches in m'pocket!"

TRY AGAIN

The farmer and his wife carried a milk churn into the Fakenham bank and took it up to the counter.

"What with all them barglaries abowt we thowt we'd better start a bank account" said the farmer. He removed the lid to show the churn was full of coins.

It took the cashier a couple of hours to count it all out. When she said how much there was the farmer looked alarmed.

"That carnt be right" he said "thass 'bowt £15 tew short."

Suddenly his wife went red. "Yew know what we're bin an' done, dunt yer?" she said.

"We're gone an' bort the wrong churn."

SUBTLE TIP

The verger acted as a guide for a tour of the village church. He gave a detailed history of the fine building.

One visitor was about to leave without so much as offering a tip or putting anything on the collection plate.

As he reached the gate he heard the verger call out: "Scuse me, ole partner. If yew should find yew hent got yar wallet when yew git hoom, jist yew remember yew dint tearke it out here."

HELPFUL SORT

Stanley got up to answer a knock at the door. A stranger stood there.

"Does Bertie Parker live here?"

"No, he dunt."

"Well would you happen to know if he lives in this street?"

"Yis, he dew live in this street."

"Would you happen to know at what number?"

"No – but that'll be on the door."

Gert: "Wuz that Horry Smythe un only child?"

Florrie: Yis – an' he still wunt his father's fearvrit!"

TAKING THE RISE

Old Charlie was receiving only nine shillings a week for working on the farm. The master approached him one morning and said: "I think you deserve a rise, Charlie. You can draw another shilling a week."

"Thankyer, marster. I'll think it over."

Next day Charlie went to the master and said: "If thass orl the searme ter yew, I dunt think I'll tearke that rise."

"Why ever not, Charlie? You put in a lot of hours here."

"Well, marster, thass like this here....if I miss harf a day, look how much more munny I'll hatter lose."

THAT ALL DEPEND

Old John was busy trimming his hedge when a stranger came up and asked him how long it would take to walk into the village.

"I carnt rightly say" said John. The stranger marched off in a huff. Then he heard John call him back.

"Reckun that'll tearke yew abowt five minutes" he declared.

"Well, why on earth could you not have told me that in the first place, my good man?" retorted the stranger sharply.

"Well, bor," explained John, "I dint know then how farst yew wuz a'goin' ter walk."

WICKET WIT

A young cricketer with public school experience moved to a new area in Norfolk and was picked to play in the big local derby against the neighbouring village.

The game was away and he made his own way there. He met a rustic leaning on the gate to the field of combat.

"Should be a close one, what?"

"Dunt reckun so atorl....we'll marder yer."

"Jolly well see about that, my good fellow! Tell me, who scores most of your runs?"

"Marster Jenkins, the cowman's boy. Allus good fer fifty."

"And who, may I ask, takes most of your wicket?"

"Why, I dew."

"You? At your age? An opening bowler...?"

"Blarst me, no bor – I'm the umpire!"

JUST ASKING

Amos splashed out and took his wife to the pictures in Norwich. During the interval he went to get them an ice cream each. In doing so he trod rather heavily on the toes of a posh lady further along the row. She scowled and muttered.

On his return Amos was about to pass the same lady when he asked: "Excuse me, my bewty, did I jam on yar toes minnit or tew back?"

Expecting an apology the lady said with some indignation: "Yes, you most certainly did."

"Oh, good," said Amos. "I hev got the right row arter all."

Gert: "How dew I avoid gittin' stiff in the joints?"
Florrie: " Thass easy ... jist stay owt on'em!"

TAKING CARE

There had been a hosepipe ban and all the gardens in the village looked very parched. All except old John's garden.

The man from the water board was rather suspicious as he called to remind John he could not use the mains water for his garden.

"Dunt yew fret, bor" John told him. "Thass like this here – when we're got pletty we use it sparingly. So when we hent got enny, we're allus got some."

NUMBERS GAME

Many years ago an inspector paid a call at a Norfolk village school. Those were the days when the head-master got paid according to how much he had taught his pupils.

The inspector came into the classroom and said to the headteacher "I'll give your class a little test on numbers." He took a bit of chalk, went to the blackboard and said: "Would some boy or girl give me a number please."

Billy Jones shouted out "63, sir" The inspector turned round and wrote on the board 36. He looked at the class but nobody spoke or flickered an eyelid.

The inspector turned to the headteacher and said "I'll try again. Can someone else give me a number?"

Mary Parker, sitting in the back row, stood up and said "59, sir" He turned round and wrote 95 on the board. Again he looked at the class. Again nobody moved or spoke. With a sigh of exasperation he said to the headteacher "Well, you've got a pretty poor lot here, but I'll give them one more chance. Right, can anyone else give me a number?"

Little Sammy Starling, sitting in the front row, jumped up and shouted "33, marster – and dew yew beggar that one abowt!"

WASTE NOT....

A young lad turned up at the village shop just before closing time on Saturday evening.

"Toylet roll, please mister."

The kindly old shopkeeper took one down from the shelf and handed it over.

First thing Monday morning the boy was there as the door was being unlocked. He had the toilet roll under his arm. He strode to the counter and thrust the roll towards the shopkeeper...

"Mum say, kin yew tearke it back – company dint come."

TASTY MORSEL

The bell rang for the end of playtime and the children raced back into school. Next lesson was arithmetic.

A rather backward pupil was singled out to answer questions about fractions, much to the obvious delight of his colleagues.

"Now, boy," said the teacher, "which would you prefer – a third of a cake or a fifth of a cake?"

The boy replied without hesitation: "Fifth of a cearke, sar!"

The teacher was very cross and demanded to know the reason for such an answer. The reply was again rapidly forthcoming:

"Please, sar, to tell yew the truth, I ent tew keen on cearke!"

LAST RITES

The tearful children were holding a funeral service in the back garden for their recently-demised hamster.

As they lowered him into his final resting place a small boy closed his eyes and said solemnly: "In the nearme o' the Father, the Son – and in the hole he goest. Amen"

Gert: "Kin yew spell Mississippi?"
Florrie: "Dew yew mean the river or the state?"

THE RIGHT PRICE

A farmer, his wife and eldest son George went away for a holiday after harvest. They left Billy in charge. He was none too bright.

The following day a neighbouring farmer paid a call, accompanied by his daughter. "Can I speak to your parents?"

"No, they hev gone away fer the weekend."

"Can I speak to George, then?"

"No, he're gone with them. They left me in charge, kin I help?"

"Well, your brother George has made my daughter pregnant and I want to know what you are going to do about it."

Billy scratched his head, looked very serious and thought for a minute.

"I carnt rightly help yer. I know how much Father charge fer th'ole bull – but I dunt know how much he charge fer George."

GOOD REMEDY

Percy went in for pig keeping. He had four sows and a boar.

Come the spring and the old boar wouldn't do his job. Percy rang the vet and he sent some tablets round. They worked a treat. The boar performed splendidly.

Come next spring and the boar was again in a reluctant mood. Percy rang the vet.

"Now larst year yew sent me some tablets… kin I hev a few more?"

"Well, how big were they?"

"Oh, I carnt remember."

"What colour were they, then?"

"I carnt remember… " There was a long silence then Percy said: "But they tearste a bit like aniseed."

TRUE COLOURS

On reaching the age of 70 a Norfolk maiden aunt turned her thoughts to the inevitable. She decided to make arrangements for her funeral.

"I hent never bin beholden ter ennyone in my life and I ent gorter start now" she mused.

Off she went to see the village undertaker. She was invited to select the lining material for the coffin. The undertaker said: "We normally bury the married women with a deep purple lining, but unmarried women like yourself usually have a nice piece of white taffeta."

The old dear thought for a while. "I tell yew what" she said eventually, "yew kin use the white taffeta, but kin yew trim th'edges wi' papple jist ter let 'em know I hed my moments!"

A little bit o' Squit

Arthur and Jack were busy picking apples when Arthur's ladder slipped, bringing him crashing to the ground.
Jack ran to his aid, shouting: "Hev yew hat yarself, bor?"
"I dunno" replied Arthur.
"I carnt speak yit!"

PRIZE REMARKS

Harry won a goat in a raffle at the local fete. A few weeks later his mate Charlie called to ask how the goat was getting on.

"He's gittin' on orryte" said Harry, rather mysteriously.

"Where hev yew put'im?" asked Charlie.

"In the bedroom allonger my missus."

"Cor, blarst me!" exclaimed Charlie. "What 'bowt the smell?"

"Tell yer the truth," said Harry, "Th'ole goot dunt fare ter mind that a mite!"

PLAYING BY EAR

A farmer in the village was a good sort willing to help anyone. Unfortunately he was almost stone deaf.

Living nearby was a cattle drover who was usually hard up and on the cadge. One day he met the farmer and shouted at him: "Lend us sixpence, ole partner!"

The farmer put his hand to his other ear and said: "What dew yew say?"

Going round the other side the drover shouted: "Lend us half a crown, ole partner!"

The farmer shook his head.

"Yew're got the wrong lug. Go yew round tew the tanner side."

TIME FLIES

It was a bit of a puzzle to regulars at The Eradicated Coypu. For several nights Ezra had been in – and he stopped to play cards and dominoes and to sink a few pints.

It was most unlike his wife to allow him such luxuries. Bill thought he'd ask how she was.

"Oh," said Ezra, "She's in horspital."

"Sorry tew hear that, ole bewty. How long hev she bin there?"

"Well, bor," said Ezra, "in three weeks she'll he'bin there nearly a month."

LEAD STORY

Obadiah lived in a caravan. One day the local policeman saw a dog tied to the caravan and asked Obadiah if he had got a licence.

"No, that I hent – and I hent got the munny ter buy one neither."

The policeman told him he'd have to get one. Later that day Obadiah turned up at the policeman's house and produced a licence.

"You told me this morning you had no money, so where have you got it from all of a sudden?"

"I sold the dawg."

MATCHING PAIR

Mabel decided to change her rather ancient Morris Minor and took a fancy to a little orange Fiat from the village garage.

She wanted to show off her new motor to her friend Ada and so invited her for a ride into town to do a bit of shopping. Half way there the car stopped. Mabel couldn't get it to start again.

They both got out and opened up the front bonnet to see if they could spot what was wrong.

"Oh, Mabel" said Ada, "Reckun yew've lorst the engine."

"Never mind," said Mabel, "There's another one in the back."

Gert: "I met a mawther yisty I hent sin fer twetty year."

Florrie: "Thass noffin – I met a feller larst week I hent never sin afore in my life!"

SIGN LANGUAGE

An elderly lady of sound means was interviewing a young Norfolk girl with a view to engaging her as a domestic servant.

"Well, Audrey, I think you'll suit me very well, provided you always remember I am a lady of very few words. So if I beckon you with my finger like this... you will know that I mean come here."

"Thass orryte, ma'm" said Audrey cheerfully. "An' if I shearke my skull like this... yew'll know I ent a'comin'!"

CITY LIGHTS

A village lad was making his first visit after dark to the big city of Norwich. He was captivated by the sight of the castle in all its floodlit glory.

As he stood admiring, a lady of the night edged towards him in her high-heels and fur coat. She didn't get any reaction, so she clicked her heels on the pavement. Still no response.

So she tugged his overalls and whispered seductively "Dew yew want a bit?"

His eyes still aloft, the lad replied: "Blarst me! What are they gorter knock it down?"

FOOD FOR THOUGHT

An old countryman was very ill in bed and hadn't been allowed anything to eat for several days.

Then the doctor called and after a lengthy examination he told the wife her husband wouldn't last much longer so he might have anything he liked to eat.

After the doctor had gone the woman called up the stairs: "Fred, doctor say yew kin hev ennything yew like ter eat."

The old man called back with something approaching delight: "Cor, blarst me, I'd wholly like some o'that there ham yew're bin a'cookin' down there. That smell bewtiful."

To which came the sharp retort: "Yew carnt he'that. Thass fer yar funeral."

ALL OF A FLUTTER

Three country vicars were having trouble with bats in their churches. They met over coffee to discuss what progress was being made.

"I put all mine in a cardboard box and took them miles away" said the first. "Unfortunately, they beat me back to the church."

"I rang the bells non-stop for five hours" said the second. "But the only result of that was to make me deaf."

"I hev got rid o'mine" said the third, a true Norfolkman. His colleagues were bursting to know the secret.

"Well, orl I dun wuz baptise 'em and confarm 'em. I hent seen 'em since!"

FINE TRIBUTE

Shortly after his arrival in a new rural parish, the vicar was asked to conduct a funeral service.

He announced: "I am very sorry that I cannot pay tribute to the deceased as I did no know him. But if any of you would like to say a few words, please feel free to do so."

There was complete silence in the little village church. The new vicar tried again. "Now, please do not be shy. I'm sure there must be someone who would like to say a kindly word about our dear departed friend."

Another long silence. Suddenly a voice from the back muttered:
"His brother wuz wass."

Gert: Hev yar ole man got wunner them things fer fixin' jobs round the house? "
Florrie: "Yis – he corl it a chequebook!"

FAMILY TIES

A Norfolk boy lived at home with his parents in the country. He was a quiet sort and so it came as a bit of a surprise when he arrived back at the house with a young lady on his arm one Sunday afternoon.

"Mum! Dad!" he called. "Come and meet Lucy! We're walkin' out tergether, an' if thing go orryte we'll be gittin' married."

His father took him to one side. "Come here, boy" he said and led him into the scullery.

"Yew carnt marry har."

"Why nut?"

"Cors she's yar sister."

The boy was most upset and didn't want any tea. In fact he moped all round the house for several weeks.

A few months later, just as Mother was again preparing the Sunday tea, the boy arrived home with another girl on his arm. He beamed proudly.

"Mum! Dad! This here is Mabel, she's my new galfriend. We're walkin' out tergether an' if evrathing go orryte, we're gorn ter git married."

"Come here, boy" said Father and wheeled him into the scullery.

"Yew carnt marry har."

"But whyever nut?"

"Cors she's yar sister!"

This time the boy was beyond consolation. He sat on his own in the front room without a word to his parents for over a week. Eventually his mother took him a cup of tea and asked what was the matter.

"I'm right fed up" he moaned.

"What are yew fed up abowt?"

"Well, every time I bring a nice gal hoom and say I'm gorn ter marry har Father tearke me inter the scullery and say 'yew carnt marry har' and I say 'why nut?' and he say 'cors thass yar sister!' That git on my wick."

His mother gave him a long lingering look and then said: "Oh...yew dunt want ter tearke no notice o'him. He ent no relation o'yars."

A little bit o' Squit

Arthur had forgotten to take off his boots before stepping indoors. His houseproud wife was nagging him mercilessly.

"I had a dozen proposals before yours, Arthur Baker," she cried scornfully, "and all from much smarter chaps than you."

"Reckun they wuz," said Arthur quietly.

"They dint marry yew."

NORFOLK AIR

Jacob had to move from his beloved countryside in later years to live with his daughter in London. He couldn't acclimatise to life in the big city. He fell ill and it soon became clear he had reached his final innings. The family gathered round the bed.

"What can we do for you?" they asked.

"Th'only thing what'll dew me enny good now is a drop o' Norfolk air" murmured the old man.

"Don't you fret" said son-in-law Fred. "I'll see to that."

Next day Fred got his bike out and set off for Norfolk. He reached Norwich Cattle Market on the Saturday morning. There he let the wind out of his tyres, pumped them up again and headed back to London.

Opening his front door he took the bike inside and carried it up the stairs.

"Here comes the boy Fred" they cried. "You'll soon be all right now, Jacob."

Fred bent down, unscrewed the valve and let all the wind out of the tyre. Old Jacob propped himself up with difficulty, took one whiff – and passed away.

"Oh dear" exclaimed his daughter. "I don't understand that. I thought it would do him some good."

"Yes" said Fred, "it's a great pity I got that puncture in Colchester."

Gert: "Dew strong drink mearke yew see dubble?

Florrie: "Yis – but that dew help me feel single!"

USING HIS HEAD

Amos was up before the local magistrates. He had hit the road foreman on the head with his shovel after an argument as to how a stretch of village road should be repaired to prevent a recurring puddle every time it rained.

The chairman of the bench asked Amos why he had hit the foreman on the head.

"Well, yar honour, we wunt a'gettin' nowhere, so I thowt thass where the trubbel might lie!"

BEYOND THE PAIL

A lad from the country, where the lavatory was at the top of the garden, joined the army. He was stationed at very modern barracks. His first letter home read:

"Dear Dad, This is the life. Orl mod cons. Flush toylets etc. When I come hoom on leave I'll dew away wi' our ole petty at top o' the garden an' we'll hev a modern one."

He duly arrived home on leave. On entering the garden gate he threw a hand grenade into the small building which went up in a cloud of dust. At the same time his father opened the front door and said: "Yes shunt he'dun that, boy... yar mother wuz in there."

When the old girl emerged from the rubble, covered in dust, straw, odd pieces of brick and torn up sheets of paper, the boy said most contritely: "I'm wholly sorry, Mum."

She replied quietly: "Wuh, that wunt yar fault, my boy. That must he'bin suffin' I ett."

NEWS BEET

In the early days of the second world war two farm labourers were pulling sugar beet on a large open field in driving wind and pouring rain.

One of them had happened to see a newspaper before coming to work. He said to his partner: "I see in the EDP them ole Jarmans hev gone inter Warsaw."

About an hour later as they reached the end of the row the other tugged at his coat collar, gazed up at the brooding skies and remarked: "Well, they hent got much of a day fer it."

Gert: "Dew yew use wine in the kitchen?"

Florrie: "Yis – an' I hev bin known ter put some inter the grub!"

HALF THE BATTLE

Old Jimmy saved up to buy a bike. He told his pals on the farm: "Blarst, now I kin hoss over ter Swaffham ter see my sister on Sundays."

On the Monday morning they naturally asked how he'd got on. "Well, by the time I git ter Dereham I wuz proper wore out, so I tanned round an' come streart hoom agin."

"But thass only harf way" they said.

"I know," said Jimmy with a smile, "I'll hatter dew th'uther harf next week."

COVER PLAN

The farmer's maid refused to get up. The farmer, thinking she was ill, sent for the doctor.

"Now, what's the matter, Mary?"

"Ent noffin the matter."

"Well, why don't you get up then?"

"They owe me two months wages – an' I dunt git up till they pay up."

The doctor smiled. "Oh, is that all. Well, shift over – they've owed me a bill for over two years!"

Gert: "Woss that boy Charlie a'gorn ter be when he pass orl them exams?"

Florrie: "Reckun he'll be a penshuner!"

DIFFERENT TUNE

An old farmer was dying. His wife and a few neighbours were sitting by the bed.

"I owe Farmer Brown five quid" whispered the old farmer.

His wife shrugged: "There he go, ramblin' agin."

After a lengthy silence the old boy started to whisper again: "Farmer Harvey owe me ten quid."

At this wife said triumphantly: "There he go agin – sensible ter the larst!"

DOORSTEP QUOTA

While the rise of the supermarket has meant the end of many rounds, the cheery milkman is still a welcome figure on the Norfolk scene, especially in rural areas. As he often calls before householders are up and about, the note on the doorstep remains a key means of communication. Here are some classics that don't quite mean what they say:

"Milkman, please close the gate behind you because the birds keep pecking the tops off the milk."

"Leave one extra pint. If this note blows away, please knock."

"Please leave an extra pint of paralysed milk."

"Please leave an extra pint of semi-skilled milk."

"No milk today. Please do not leave milk at No 14 as he is dead until further notice."

"No milk, thank you. We are away for the weekend which is why I am hiding this note under the doormat so that nobody finds out."

"Milk is needed for the baby. Father unable to supply it."

"Money on the table. Wife in bed. Please help yourself."

Milkmen prepare for their rounds, looking forward to the odd amusing note or two.

SURPRISE TONIC

A rather deaf old lady, whose sight was not too good, complained of feeling unwell. Her grand-daughter called the doctor.

As he left the grand-daughter, raising her voice, said: "Well, Grandma, how are you feeling now?"

"A little better. It was nice of the wikker ter call."

"But Grandma, that was the doctor, not the vicar... ."

"Well, blarst me!" said the old lady. "I was jist a'thinkin' he wuz a bit familiar!"

WIND DIRECTION

A motorist taking a short cut through country lanes in Norfolk came to a main road where he found a sign-post to Norwich. But it was pointing in the opposite direction to what he had expected.

An old man, clearly a local, wandered towards him and said: "Dunt yew tearke enny notice o'that ole pust – thass loose.

"When the wind's in the east Norwich lay over there. When thass in the west Norwich lay over here....."

BACK TO WORK

A Norfolk farmer was waiting for his men to arrive for work on a very frosty morning.

One chap had to walk two miles across the fields. The farmer asked him why he was late.

"That bloomin' footpath wuz so slippery evra time I took a step forrard I skidded back two."

"Well," said the farmer, "how did you get here, then?"

The chap replied: "Blarst, I tanned round an' went hoom."

DEFIANT END

An elderly Norfolk couple had led a cat and dog existence and hadn't spoken to each other for years.

The husband fell ill and lay dying. His wife, anxious for a reconciliation before it was too late, decided to make the first move.

She went upstairs to the old man's bedside and, breaking the long silence between them, whispered: "George, where dew yew want ter be buried?"

The answer came back without hesitation and in a voice full of malice:

"On top o'yew!"

FOWL PLAY

Charlie called at the village shop to buy a dozen eggs.

As the shopkeeper went to serve him Charlie exclaimed: "Hold yew hard! I want the ones what the yeller-legged hens lay."

With a puzzled look the shopkeeper told Charlie that if he had any way of telling which ones they were, he could pick them out himself.

Charlie did – he picked out the biggest dozen he could find.

HIGH TIDE

George and Billy went for a day out at the seaside. They ate their sandwiches on the beach. Billy finished drinking his cold tea and then wandered down to the sea to fill his bottle with water.

"What are yew a'doin'?" said George.

"Well, my missus hent sin the sea fer years and I thowt I'd tearke some onnit hoom for har."

"Yew silly ole fewl" said George, "when the tide come in that'll bust the bottle!"

Gert: "Did they call the doctor when young Sam swollered a coin? "

Florrie: "No – they sent fer the parson. He kin git munny outer ennybody!"

A little bit o' Squit

An item on a Norfolk restaurant menu was marked "The Chef's Special". Underneath it someone wrote: "So he myte be – but his grub ent up ter much!"

SLOW LEARNER

Tom won most of the prizes as usual at the local horticultural show. The vicar presented him with his cups and asked him how he did it.

"Manewer" said Tom, "good, rotten manewer."

Tom went off. The vicar turned to Tom's wife; "He is truly a marvellous gardener, but I wish you could teach him to call it fertilizer rather than manure."

"I'll dew my best, wikker" said Mabel, "but that took me thatty year ter git him ter say manewer!"

BARGAIN PRICE

It had been a bad year for potatoes but Horry grew his own and had a good crop. He decided to sell them from a little table at his front gate for 60p a pound.

A lady, a renowned bargain-hunter, looked at the price and said: "The fellow on the market is selling his at 50p a pound."

"Well," said Horry, "why dint yew buy them orff him?"

"He'd sold out" said the woman.

Back came Horry quick as a flash: "Well, I're sold out I sell 'em fer 50p a pound as well."

WE ALL MAKE....

On old carpenter working at the local doctor's house was noticed putting putty in his joints to make a good fit.

One day the doctor said: "I suppose a piece or two of putty has covered up several of your mistakes, George?"

"Yis, doctor," replied the carpenter, "an' I bet a sod or tew o' grass hev covered up savrul o' yours anorl!"

RICH REWARD

Jimmy was "backus boy" at the hall. That meant he did all the dirty, unpleasant little tasks. One day the squire came into the yard and handed Jimmy a hare he had just shot.

"Take that to the rectory, boy, and be quick about it!"

The rector was noted for being mean. Jimmy muttered to himself as he went, dragging the hare behind him: "Gotter tearke this bloomin' thing ter the parson, an' he oont gi' me noffin."

Jimmy expected to see the maid when he knocked at the back door, so he said in surly tones: "Squire say I're gotter gi' yew this." To his surprise, it was the rector who opened the door.

"Now, Jimmy," he said reproachfully, "that's not the way to present a gift. I'll show you how to do it correctly. Just give me the hare. I'll knock on the door and you open it."

So he knocked on the door and when Jimmy opened it the rector said: "Please sir, squire sends you this and hopes you will kindly accept it."

Jimmy replied with a grin: "Well, thank yew, my little man – here's harf a crown fer yar trubble!"

A little bit o' Squit

Billy was busy helping with a few household chores.

"Why are yew cleanin' th'inside o'them windows, but nut the outside?" asked his missus.

"Well, thass like this here," answered Billy.

"That way we kin look out but them outside carnt look in."

MRS BLUNT

A man wanted to be "buried decent" and to this end he had his coffin made some years before it was likely to be needed and kept it in the front room.

During a serious illness his clergyman paid a visit. The patient told him all was ready …"Dew yew go an' see that there corffin." The vicar did so and told the man's wife it was indeed a very handsome coffin.

"Yis, I spooz thass orryte" said the old lady. "But I'll be glad ter see the back onnit. That dew clutter the plearce up so."

BACK TO FRONT

Horry and his missus were getting on an excursion train bound for Yarmouth at Ellingham station when they were told they wouldn't have to change at Beccles as usual.

"They're gorn ter hitch this here train on ter th'uther one" explained the porter.

Sure enough, at Beccles the Waveney Valley carriages were shunted on to the rear of the Yarmouth train. The only thing was this meant that those facing the engine were now sitting back to the engine.

"Thass a rummun" said Horry. "I're bin a'sittin' opposite yew – an' now yew're sittin' opposite ter me… ."

GOOD OFFER

Charlie was riding on the bus in Yarmouth, smoking his usual Park Drive when the conductor woman came along and politely asked him to put his fag out as smoking was allowed only on the top deck.

Charlie didn't quite understand and continued puffing. The conductress returned rather annoyed that her authority had been flouted and tapped him on the shoulder.

"Dew yew want ter git me inter trubble?" she asked.

Quick as a flash came Charlie's retort: "Blarst yis – what time dew yew leave orff?"

QUICK THINKING

When National Service was in force a young man from rural Norfolk was called up. He pleaded very poor eyesight. Indeed, he failed all the usual tests. Finally, the examiner held up a dustbin lid and said: "Tell me, lad, what's this?"

The lad blinked and replied: "Well, ole bewty, thass either a two-bob bit or half-a-crown."

That did the trick.

He was not accepted – and went off to celebrate with a trip to the cinema in Norwich.

He hadn't been sitting there long when, to his horror, the examiner came in and sat next to him they recognised each other

Quick as a flash, the rejected conscript exclaimed: "Am I on the right bus for Corpusty?"

HEAVENS ABOVE

Ezra was an odd-job man on a Norfolk farm. He was constantly bustled by all and sundry, particularly by the farmer.

Ezra died and went above. Several years later the farmer took the same route, and after passing through the golden gates he bumped into Ezra.

"How are yew a'gittin' on, ole partner?" he asked.

Ezra fixed him with a serious stare and said: "Dew yew git on wi' yar own tasks, marster. I'm on the staff up here!"

Gert: "Old Charlie's gittin' excited 'bowt the flower show."

Florrie: "Yis – thass his regglar attack o' wisteria!"

A little bit o' Squit

Lady of the manor: "Has anyone offered you work?"

Tramp: "Only once, ma'am. Other than that, I have met with nothing but kindness."

GOOD WHIFF

A true story from Norfolk in the days before mains water.

A lad was sent home from school with a note demanding that he be washed. The indignant mother sent him straight back with this written reply:

"Deer Miss, Yew hev sent our Billy hoom because yew say he smell. Well, let me tell yew I send him ter school ter be larnt not smelt. Anyway, he smell jist like his father smell.

"But there, yew bein' an' ole maid, I dunt spooz yew know what a good man smell like."

TOUGH TASK

A shortage of jobs in the town meant the boy had to look for work on a farm.

The foreman told him to milk a cow, handing over stool and bucket. An hour later the boy returned dirty and sweaty. He had the bucket in one hand and a broken stool in the other.

"Gittin' the milk wuz easy," he explained. "Hardest part wuz a'mearkin' th'ole cow sit on the stewl."

IN A SPIN

A top showbusiness agent passed a building site and saw a man do five back somersaults and a head spin.

The agent called out: "Brilliant! I'll book you for the summer season at Yarmouth."

The man replied: "Yew'll hev ter book Paddy as well. He's the one who burned my backside wi' his blow-torch."

RETURN TRIP

A farmer engaged a new hand whose first job was to take a horse and cart into the field to fetch two loads of cattle beet out of the clamp and take them to the barn for winter feeding.

The farmer thought the chap was a long time coming back, but reckoned he had missed him when he brought the first load.

However, the lad turned up and the farmer asked if indeed this was the first load.

"Blarst, no," he replied "thass my second load. I'm now a'gorn back arter the fust one."

PASTY PUZZLE

The village church choir went on its annual outing to the Norfolk seaside. The new young vicar, thinking it would be a treat, ordered oyster pasties for high tea instead of the usual fish and chips.

Old Henry, who had never seen such things before, gazed at them for a minute or two. Then he carefully took the top off one on his plate and peered inside suspiciously.

After poking it with his fork, he called: "Hi, parson, dew yew come here a minnit. Suffin's died in my bun."

EYES HAVE IT

Two young shepherds were rehearsing for the Nativity play. They came in, knelt down – and said nothing.

Teacher suggested they might think of something nice to say about baby Jesus. So they set out to try again.

They came in, knelt down – and one said: "He's a bew'ful little boy, an', dew yew know, I think he're got yar eyes."

Gert: "How old dew yew reckun Norridge Cathedral is?"

Florrie: "Dunno – but thass bin there as long as I kin remember."

SLIGHT DELAY

Two Norfolk pensioners were recalling their second world war experiences.

"Horry, dew yew remember them pills they useter give us in the Air Force ter keep our minds orff the mawthers?"

"Come ter think onnit, I dew."

"Well, I reckun mine are beginnin' ter work!"

CABBAGE COUNT

A Norfolk gardener kept his horticultural cards close to his chest.

A neighbour peered over the fence and asked: "How many cabbages he' yew got planted out there?"

"Harf as menny as I want."

"Wuh, how the davil menny dew yew want, then?"

"Twice as menny as woss there now."

RIGHT POLICY

Billy's bonfire got out of hand and his garden shed was burnt down. He went to see his insurance agent in the hope of collecting the money for it.

The agent explained it didn't work like that: "You have to fill in a claim form and then an assessor will call and value the damage. And in any case we don't pay out cash, we replace the property."

Billy thought for a minute or two.

"In that case," he said, "yew'd better cancel that there policy on my missus!"

> ## A little bit o' Squit
>
> Norfolk girl's father: "Look here, ole partner, we turn the lights out at harf past ten in this house."
>
> Young man: "Well, thass bloomin' nice o'yer!"

HE TWIGGED IT

A London businessman on holiday in rural Norfolk was chatting to a village resident. The conversation came round to bird life and habits.

Pointing to a rook's nest high in the trees beyond the church, the local said: "Dew yew know, sar, them there rooks only use two sorts o'twigs ter build thar nests?"

"Most interesting," replied the visitor. "Would you know what sort they are/"

"Yis," answered the local, "straight 'uns an' bent 'uns."

FEATHERED BONUS

A Norfolk farmer sent his nephew a crate of chickens. The box burst open just as the boy started to take them out.

Next day he wrote to his uncle: "I chased 'em through my neighbour's farmyard, but only got 13 of them back."

Answered the farmer: "Yew did orryte. I only sent six."

INFLATED TALE?

Charlie was showing a party of tourists round Yarmouth. He pointed out the spot where Lord Nelson supposedly threw a gold sovereign across the River Yare.

"That's impossible" said a tourist. "No-one could throw a coin that far."

"Ah, but yew hev ter remember," explained Charlie, "Munny went a rare lot farther in them days."

Gert: "That Ethel's a bit on the slow side, ent she?"

Florrie: "Yis – that tearke har a week ter git rid o' a 24-hour virus!"

PORK AND RIDE

A charming farmyard scene from my mid-Norfolk home village of Beeston, thought to have been taken in the 1930s. This "squealbarrow" interlude has been added to an impressive collection of old photographs at Litcham Museum.

NOWHERE TO RUN

The Norfolk farmer was complaining to Hector, one of his workers, about his habitual tardiness.

"Strange," he said, "you're always late and you live just across the road. Charlie lives three miles away and yet he's always on time."

"Noffin' strange 'bowt that atorl" replied Hector.

"If Charlie's late in the mornin', he kin hurry. If I'm late, I'm here."

BULL RUSH

A commuter moved to the Norfolk countryside.

Desperate to catch a train, he called out to a farmer busy tending his cows along the lane: "Hey, Grandpa, is it OK with you if I take a short cut across your field? I really must catch the 8.15."

The farmer smiled and replied: "Dew yew go ahid, young marster – but if my bull see yew, reckun yew might catch the 7.45."

A LITTLE LATE

Norfolk parents with their young boy arrived at the church for the christening.

The vicar, expecting to see an infant in arms, was rather surprised.

"And where is your baby son, Mrs Jones?" he asked.

She pointed to her five-year-old child: "Thass my boy woss got ter be done, sar."

"But aren't you a little late?"

"Ever so sorry, reverend," said the mother, "but my ole man hed an awful job a'gittin' the motor ter start."

HOME EARLY

The annual outing from the village pub to Yarmouth was drawing to a close. Some of the party were finding their way back to the bus when one of them noticed a darts team regular sprawled out on the beach clearly the worse for drink.

"Wuh, there's ole Harry!" he exclaimed. "We'd better lift 'im inter the bus."

He was still tipsy when the bus arrived home so it was decided to rouse him under the village pump.

"Now are yew fit enuff ter walk hoom?" they asked.

"Walk hoom?" Harry bellowed. "I wunt even on this here bloomin' outin'. I wuz on a week's holiday wi' my missus!"

Gert: "Woss the best way o' gittin' yar old man tew dew suffin'?"
Florrie: "Thass easy – tell 'im he's too old ter dew it!"

KIND WORDS

Martha's husband died and she decided to put an announcement in the local paper. She told the girl in the office she wanted to keep it as short as possible.

"Jist put 'Horry Grimble dead'" she suggested.

"Actually, my dear, you can have up to six words for the same price. Would you like to add anything?"

Martha pondered for a while and then said: "Right, kin yew add: 'Ferret fer sale'?"

HELPFUL SIGN

A stranger walked into a Norfolk village shop. He saw a sign reading: "Beware of the Dawg."

He spotted an old sheep dog sprawled out on the floor, fast asleep.

"Is that the dog referred to on your sign?" he asked the shopkeeper.

"Reckun that is" came the reply.

"Well, it's hard to believe that dog is dangerous. Why on earth did you put that sign up?"

"Well, since I put that sign up people hev stopped trippin' over him."

TRICKY CUSTOMER

Horry was always being teased by the other village lads.

One of their favourite games was to show how stupid he was by giving him the choice of picking a 20p piece or a 10p piece.

He always chose the 10p piece, sending the bullies into fits of mocking laughter.

"He's thick!" they yelled. "He pick the 10p cors thass bigger!"

The local shopkeeper watched this trick being carried out many times before taking Horry to one side.

"I'm sure you must know 10p isn't worth as much as 20p just because it's bigger?" he queried.

"Cors I dew" beamed Horry, "but if stop pickin' the 10p, wuh, they'd stop playin' the trick."

CLEAR MEANING

The young Norfolk lad was caught by his teacher saying a very naughty word.

"Peter," she scolded, "you must not use that word. Where on earth did you hear it?"

"Please miss, my dad said it" said the boy.

"Well, that doesn't matter. I don't suppose for one moment you even know what it means."

"Oh yis I dew....that mean the car wunt start."

MARKET FORCES

A teacher in a Norfolk village school received the following letter from the mother of one of her pupils:

"Deer Miss. Please dunt give Charlie no more hoomwork. That sum abowt how long that'd tearke a man ter walk 40 times rownd Swaffham Markit cawsed his father ter miss a whole day's work.

"An' then when he'd walked it, yew marked the bloomin' sum wrong."

IDEAL COUPLE

An elderly widow and widower on the Norfolk coast had been dating for five years.

Charlie finally asked Mary to marry him and she said yes.

But next morning Charlie couldn't remember what her answer had been. In desperation, he decided to phone her.

"This is very embarrassin'," he began, "but when I asked yew ter marry me yisty....well, this mornin', I jist carnt remember what yar answer wuz."

"Oh, I'm wholly glad yew called" replied Mary.

"I remember sayin' yis ter someone – but I couldn't remember who it wuz."

Gert: "I reckun Mabel's the sort o' friend yew kin depend on."

Florrie: "Yis – allus around when she need yew!"

FAST THINKING

The vicar's wife peered out of the window and saw a familiar figure coming up the garden path.

She called to her husband: "William, here comes that dreadful bore Mrs Claypole. I suppose she's here to discuss the most recent sins of our parishioners. You'd better disappear to your study upstairs."

The vicar did so.

After nearly an hour of listening and nodding, his wife excused herself, went to let the cat out and took it to the kitchen for a saucer of milk.

William, noting the end of conversation and hearing the door open and shut, assumed the coast was clear. He called out over the banister: "I'll be down in a minute, dear, now that dreadful bore has gone."

Unflustered, his wife, in sweet, dulcet tones, called up the stairs: "Oh, but you must come down at once, William. That dreadful bore went over an hour ago. Mrs Claypole is here now."

NO REPEATS

A Norfolk vicar was invited to speak at the Rotary Club's monthly lunch. A reporter from the local newspaper was present at the meal.

After his talk, full of light-hearted anecdotes, the vicar begged the reporter not to print too many of his tales as he wished to use them at future local functions.

To the clergyman's utter dismay when he opened the newspaper a few days later he found the reporter had written: "The vicar made an excellent speech – but most of the stories he told cannot be repeated here."

HOLY WATER

A clergyman taking over temporary Sunday duty asked his Norfolk parish clerk to place a glass of water in the upstairs pulpit so he could drink it before starting his sermon.

After the service, the minister remarked: "You know, John, that might have been gin for all the congregation could tell."

On the next occasion he discovered to his horror that it was gin. Came a whisper from old John below: "I took the hint, sar. I took the hint!"

SMOKE SIGNAL

A Norfolk lad who looked about ten was leaning against a wall smoking a cigarette when an elderly lady came up to him.

"Does your father know you smoke, little boy?" she inquired.

The boy stood open-mouthed. Then he took a few more puffs and looked her up and down.

"Yew're a married woman, aren't yer?" he said.

"I most certainly am," came the response.

"Well," snapped the boy, "dew yar husband know yew talk ter strange men?"

TABLE MANNERS

Some years ago, when tourism was new to this part of East Anglia, the village café was under pressure due to a sudden influx of visitors brought in by a bout of hot weather.

The owner-cum-waitress was getting rather harassed. Most waited patiently, but one "furriner", who'd been jiffling about and drumming his fingers on the table, blurted out: "Don't we get served?"

Rather red in the face, the woman had an immediate response. "Sum dew. Sum dunt. Yew dunt!"

The man left.

A little bit o' Squit

Two old Norfolk anglers, sitting on a bridge, their lines in the water, made a bet as to who would catch the first fish.

On getting a bite, one became so excited he fell off the bridge.

"Beggar this" said the other. "If yew're gorter dive in arter 'em, the bet's orff!"

A LOT OF BULL

The village parson was surprised to meet in a narrow lane one of his smallest Sunday School pupils driving a large cow.

"Good morning, Mary. Where are you going with that enormous beast?"

"Please sar, I'm a tearkin' ole Buttercup ter be bulled."

"Dear me, but couldn't your father do that?"

"Oh no, sar.....that must be a bull."

SHORE DOES!

An old Norfolk woman from the country went to the seaside for the first time.

She looked at the waves and then asked a friend who was with her: "Dew that allus keep a'muddlin' along like that?"

A MATTER OF ....

There had been a sudden death in the village and two Norfolk mawthers were discussing it.

"Ent that a rummun...there's ole Mrs Carter woss bin ailing fer years an' she's still alive, an' poor ole Aggie Smith wunt hardly ill a week...."

"Well, thass how that go. Some people die all of a sudden, an' some onnem live till the werry last moment."

IN AND OUT

Horry was working hard in his front garden when his old mate Fred came wandering past.

"I're jist bin ter hev a look at that Spring Show down the village hall."

"Oh, ah," said Horry, "an' what dew they charge ter go in there these days?"

"I dunt rightly know cors I dint pay, yer see."

"How'd yew manage that, ole partner?"

"I walked in backards – an' they thowt I wuz a'comin' out!"

PERFECT LINE

A couple of American servicemen were waiting for a train. They kept on telling the old Norfolk porter how they had bigger and faster trains back home.

He just got on with his work and didn't reply. They were just about to elaborate when a fast train to Yarmouth raced through, hauled by a Britannia class locomotive.

"Gee, buddy, what on earth was that?" asked one of the Americans.

"Oh," said the old porter in a very matter-of-fact way, "I reckun that wuz ole Tom dewin' a bit o'shuntin'."

DAD'S DILEMMA

A farmer came out of the yard to find a worried looking lad standing beside an overturned load of hay.

"Don't you worry, boy, I'll get a couple of my chaps to pitch it back."

"But what'll father say?"

"Come you in and have a glass of beer while they're loading up."

"But what'll father say?"

"For goodness sake, boy! Why are you worrying so much about your father?"

"Cors he's under the hay!"

Gert: "Thass wholly rewd ter tork wi' yar mouth full..."

Florrie: "Yis – an' that ent tew good when yar hid is empty either!"

TON-UP REPLY

On his 100th birthday a Norfolk countryman was interviewed by a posh reporter from the city.

"Well, Mr Higgins, I suppose you have witnessed a great many radical changes across this county in your time?"

"Yis," came the reply, "an' I hev opposed every bloomin' one onnem!"

LAD'S LOGIC

The farmer turned to the boy who was late for work again.

"Do you know what time you start work?"

"Yis …'bowt five minnits arter I git here."

"No, you silly young fool….why are you late?"

"Thass like this here, Marster. When that wuz time ter come ter work I wuz asleep. I knew that wunt no good a'comin' then….so I wearted till I woke up!"

BUILDING PLOT

A stranger lost his way in the Norfolk countryside. He stopped to ask directions of a farmer putting up a small wooden building in his field.

After listening carefully the stranger then asked the farmer what he was building.

"Well, that orl depend," came the reply. "If I kin rent it out at a good price, thass a charmin' rustic cottage.

"If I carnt – then thass a hen-house."

LOCAL LIMERICKS

There was an old vicar of Skeyton
Who parishioners thought was a right'un
For he preached: "Have no fear,
For the good Lord is near,"
But he slept every night with the light on.

There was a quack doctor from Dilham
Whose motto was "Cure 'em or kill 'em"
But his trade multiplied
For, if anyone died
He'd play very fair and not bill 'em.

A pregnant young mum from Stoke Ferry
Had a craving for sipping sweet sherry
When the baby arrived
He hiccupped and thrived....
But his nose was as red as a cherry.

There was a young fellow from Trunch
Who always ate cockles for lunch
When they said: "Boil 'em first"
He replied: "Why, they'd burst,
And I dearly love something to crunch."

An olde-worlde hangman from Fincham
Said: "Their necks dunt harf creak when I lynch 'em"
His mats said: "Cor blarst
Bor, why dint yew arst?
Yew soak 'em in oil – then yew winch 'em."

A bookie with business in Rackheath
Was really fed up to the back teeth.
When a punter came in
With another big win
His staff whipped around for a black wreath.

There was an old maid from Sea Palling
Who averred that today's youth are galling
"When I walk out at night
With my dog and flashlight
What we find in the dunes is appalling."

A granny who came from Pott Row
Went out to a Chippendales' show
Thought she got home all right
Grandad soon had a fright
When her pacemaker started to glow.

A struggling young athlete from Bintree
Was known for a smile that was wintry
When asked: "Why so grim?"
He replied: "In the gym
The floor is decidedly splintery."

There was a young lady of Sustead
Who bathed in hot milk which she trusted
Would improve her skin
But too long she stayed in
And came out smelling strongly of custard.

Gert: "Dew yar ole man still chase mawthers?"

Florrie: "Yis – but he carnt remember why!"

There was an old fellow of Cromer
Who sat on the pier reading Homer
Said: "I've been here all week
And I'm finding this Greek
Gives off quite a fishy aroma."

A lady hitchhiker from Docking
Has a method some people find shocking
For it isn't her thumb
She show as cars come
But the flesh at the top of her stocking

There was an old woman of Wymondham
Who purchased some rabbits and tymondham
They were cooked quite enough
But were covered in flough
Cos the foolish old gal hadn't skymondham.

And elderly farmhand from Flitcham
Said: "Combines? I'd willingly ditch 'em
The harvest's an art
With a horse and a cart
Just cop me the shoofs and I'll pitch 'em!"

A cow in a field down at Guist
Gave milk which was flavoured and spiced
My hart, that dew smell!
But it sells rather well
Because it is reasonably priced.

There was a young feller from Brampton
Whose bunion he feared would get stamped on
So vacations were spent
In a field in a tent
Which nobody else ever camped on.

HEAVENLY HUMOUR

A village chapel diet of three courses every Sunday, plus a Tuesday Fellowship snack if you couldn't come up with a good excuse, merely hinted at a rich seam of humour to be tapped in years to come.

Our Methodist meeting-place provided a few chuckles during those rather austere years after the second world war. Walter Ward banged on the pew and shouted "Amen!" if he agreed with the preacher. Charlie Elliott's hearing aid made strange whistling noises when he fiddled with it. "He's trying to get Luxembourg!" whispered boys at the back. Elijah Brown, all shiny buskins and Sunday boots, rattled a sweet paper loudly and glared at his pocket watch if he felt the preacher had out-stayed his welcome. The old Tortoise stove played up in winter if the wind was in the wrong direction. We prayed fervently for billowing smoke to bring proceedings to a spluttering end.

While I may have missed one or two pertinent points being expounded by animated brethren on the Swaffham Methodist Circuit, a keen theological debate outside our village shop did catch my imagination in telling fashion. Two stalwart parishioners were leaning on the railings near the post box.

One said to the other in broad Norfolk tones: "Dew yew reckon God hev a sense o' humour?"

At that precise moment a well-known busybody of the community cranked past on her sit-up-and-beg bike, her ample knees pumping, her large bosoms heaving and her big hat wobbling on her head.

The chap who'd been asked the question of the hour turned to his inquisitor and said without a hint of malice: "I think that might hev answered yar question, ole partner."

Church Entertainers – the cast of All Preachers Great and Small ready for another show in a local church. Left to right: Keith Skipper, David Woodward, Brian Patrick and Ian Prettyman.

That was one of the inspirations behind my collection of ecclesiastical chuckles shared in recent times with cheerful gatherings for presentations of All Preachers Great and Small in local churches and chapels. These affectionate tributes to those who have graced our pulpits over the years brought three of my favourite people to the fore.

David Woodward, from Frostenden, near Beccles, had the role of Parson James Woodforde, who held the living at Weston Longville, a few miles from Norwich, from May, 1776 until his death on New Year's Day in 1803. His parish is better known today for its turkey sheds and popular dinosaur park.

Brian Patrick, from Beccles, a former village school headmaster, appeared in the guise of the Rev. Benjamin Armstrong, Vicar of East Dereham from September, 1850 until he resigned through ill-health in 1888. Both venerable gentlemen of the cloth provided excerpts from their diaries, many of them spiced with humour.

Ian Prettyman, a pillar of the modern Methodist church in Lowestoft completed our troupe with musical items, singing and playing his melodeon.

I have always maintained that our churches are natural theatres and that there's no reason why the Devil should claim all the good yarns. Laughter and applause from smiling congregations all over the county, and on occasional forays into Suffolk, supported these views with relish.

I also found room for Bible stories in Norfolk dialect chosen from two delightful volumes by former Methodist minister Colin Riches – Dew Yew Lissen Hare and Orl Bewtiful An' New. Colin often drew attention to the homely but fitting illustrations used by the old lay preachers. One used to remind his hearers every spring and summer of God's providential care – "The Lord, He knew what he wuz a'doin', mearkin' rhubarb afore strawberries!"

I remember one dear old boy who arrived at our chapel on his bike with Bible and hymn book in the saddle bag. He used to offer by way of introduction: "I compare yew lot tew the contents o' a gret ole Christmas pudden', an' I am the long-handed spune woss bin sent ter stir yew up!"

Cyril Jolly, writer, raconteur and long-serving preacher from Gressenhall, sent me this little gem: At Wendling Chapel many sermons ago the preacher noticed two women in the back pew talking during the singing of a hymn. He held up his hands and stopped the singing abruptly. In the silence one of the women was heard to say: "Yis, an' I allus fry mine in lard."

Another memorable yarn to come my way concerned a travelling Norfolk preacher in the days when open-air services were common events. He arrived at the village green where a local supporter had loaned a big empty barrel for the preacher to stand on so he could be seen and clearly heard.

Hymns were sung lustily. The gathering listened attentively to the Bible reading. Another hymn and the preacher announced his text: "Lo, I am with you but soon you will see me not." Suddenly there was a loud crack and a bang as the hapless preacher disappeared into the barrel. Silent reverence gave way to rustic guffaws of laughter. Those nearby tried to retrieve the trapped preacher. It was hopeless to continue with the service, so a quick "The Day Thou Gavest, Lord, Is Ended" dismissed the meeting.

A former Bishop of Norwich, the Rt Rev Peter Nott, soon got to grips with the Norfolk way of keeping matters in perspective:

"I was taking a Communion Service in a freezing church in West Norfolk. When it was over I walked to the back of the church. My hands were completely numb with cold and I had great difficulty grasping the mug of hot coffee the churchwarden gave me.

'My goodness, your church is cold' I said.

'Oh, yes, Bishop, that is a bit parky,' said the churchwarden, 'but yew should be here when we dunt hev the heatin' on.'"

Divine humour – and here's a silver collection of my favourites from the ecclesiastical department.

Gert: "Is yar ole man lookin' around fer work?"

Florrie: "No, he carnt – he're got a stiff neck."

A little bit o' Squit

Choir member to church organist in a Norfolk village: "I reckun if yew wuz ter let us go back a bar or two so we kin git a tidy good run at it, we could jist abowt get up ter that note."

A little bit o' Squit

A Father Christmas in his Norwich grotto asked a little girl her name. She gave him a baleful stare and snorted: "I told yew in Dereham this mornin' and yew're forgotten alrid-dy!"

THE LONG SERVICE

The regular vicar was about to take his fortnight's holiday; so he called to see his friend the rector of a nearby parish. "Would you kindly take the service for me in my church next Sunday" he asked. His friend readily consented and duly turned up at the church at the appointed time. Old Isaac the dairy farmer was the only parishioner to turn up.

After waiting a while the rector said, "Well, it says in the good book, that when two, three or more are gathered together – thou shalt grant their request. But this is ridiculous, here I have a congregation of only one, do you think I should take the service?"

"Look here, master," said Isaac, "when I take a load of hay down to the bottom meadow to feed my herd and only one turns up, I feed it."

The rector thought "Well, it looks as if he wants me to take the service," which he did, for a full hour and a half.

"Was that all right?" he asked Isaac at the end.

"Look here, master," the old farmer replied. "When I take that load of hay down to the bottom meadow to feed my herd, and only one turns up, I don't give it the whole durn load!"

(*Salt on a White Plate* - Frank Etheridge)

EXCLUSIVE CLUB

Old Tom was in the habit of falling asleep in church, so the parson thought he would teach him a lesson. That Sunday morning in the middle of his sermon he could see old Tom had nodded off, so he said in a very soft voice "Everybody who wants to go to Hell....." and then he shouted very loudly.... "STAND UP!"

Old Tom woke with a start, jumped up and looked round. He could see no other members of the congregation standing. So he said: "I dunt know what we're a votin' for wikker, but that look like you and me are the only ones for it!"

Gert: "That mawther Ethel reckun she's a light eater."

Florrie: "Yis – soon's thass light, she start eatin'!"

PEAK CONDITION

Many a Norfolk farmworker made a bold fashion statement in the good old days of milking by hand. Here's emphatic proof that a cap with a peak at the back was an essential item in the cowman's wardrobe.

A little bit o' Squit

On hearing of the death of King George V, a Norfolk farmworker showed distress at the news. Then he quietly remarked: "If yew'd ha' told me afore, that wunt he' come so sudden."

TAKING A CHANCE

The wife of the churchwarden was taking her seat in the front row of the pews when she tripped and rolled over, revealing her underwear to the congregation. Seeing her predicament, the vicar stood in front of her and said: "If any man should look at this poor, unfortunate woman, may the Lord strike him blind." Charlie in the third row tuned to his friend and said: "I think I'll risk one eye."

MANY A SLIP...

The new vicar was visiting an elderly parishioner whose cottage and crockery were far from clean. Playing safe, he held the cup in his left hand to drink from the other side. "Ent that a rummun," said the dear old girl. "Yew're left-handed, jist like me!"

LOUD WHISPER

A drunk walked into church and the confessional by mistake. The priest heard him come in and sat on the other side for five minutes. Eventually he knocked on the wall. The drunk awoke, rather startled, and whispered very loudly: "Thash no good knockin' ole partner – ent no pearper thish side nyther!"

Gert: "Wuz yars a fairytale weddin'?"

Florrie: "Reckun so – if yew mean Grimm!"

A little bit o' Squit

A Norfolk farmer died suddenly and after a short while his widow announced that she was going to see a spiritualist.

Asked what good that could possibly do her, she replied: "A lot o'good. We carnt find the plearce where my husband writ down the dates fer the cow's calvings."

STAND AND DELIVER

The village parson was rather on the short side and had a stool in the pulpit upon which he stood to deliver his Sunday sermons.

One week he ascended the pulpit steps only to find the stool missing. There was nothing for it but to try to stand on tiptoe and peer over the top of the pulpit as best as he could. He announced his text: "I am the Lamp of the Lord."

From the back of the little church old Amos called out: "Well, tan yar wick up, ole partner, we carnt see yer!"

DREAM FORECAST

A Norfolk rector was visited by a lady parishioner rather early in the morning. The old lady was agitated.

"Sorry ter trubbel yew this tyme o' the mornin' Rector, but I thowt yew cood intarprat a dream I hed larst nyte. I drempt I saw my ole man – yew 'member him, dunt yer? Well, he come an' stand by m'bedside, and he did look bewtiful! He hev a crown on his hid, an' a harp in his hand, and a long, white robe on, and, oh, he did look bewtiful.

"Dew yew think that mean rain?"

HEARTFELT PRAYER

This story concerns Horry the verger in a small Norfolk parish. He had been rather poorly and it was arranged for him to visit a top specialist in London.

On his return he said to the rector:

"I am in a werry sad way, marster. I mustn't dig any more grearves or toll them bells or dew noffin what put a strean on my body. An' I want yew ter pray fer me on Sunday."

"Well, what exactly is wrong with you, Horace?"

"I hev got a floatin' kidney."

"Oh," smiled the rector. "If I should say that prayers are asked for our dear verger Horace who has a floating kidney, then I'm afraid the congregation might laugh."

"Oh, ah," mused Horry. "Oh ah. Well, congregearshun dint larf th'uther Sunday when yew prayed for loose livers."

Gert: "Dew that Ada go ter chatch ennymore?"

Florrie: "No – she's wun o'them Seventh Day Absentists."

A little bit o' Squit

Two old Norfolk boys who hadn't seen each other for the best part of some time met for a mardle.

Arthur: "Is yar sister Mary still alive, bor?"

Ernie: "Far's I know...she hent writ ter say no diffrunt."

FRANK REPLY

The local vicar called at the village school and found the little ones, aged five or so, busy painting. He approached Frank in the back row and asked what he was creating.

"Thass a pitcher o' God" came the reply.

"But nobody knows what God looks like" said the Vicar.

Frank looked up and beamed. "Well, they will do when I're dun my pitcher."

USEFUL ADVICE

The old village parson had retired and the new incumbent was biking round the parish to meet his flock. As he passed the pub he called "Good morning, gentlemen" to two old boys sipping their pints on the seat outside.

"Thass owr new parsun" say George. "Heez a rummun.. got seven kids and nuther wun on the way."

"Oh, ah" say Charlie... "He wotter wear his trowsers same way he wear his collar!"

A little bit o' Squit

Seen on a wall in Nrwch:

"DWN WTH VWLS"

AT THE DOUBLE

A Norfolk rector had as his churchwarden a chap called Ebenezer, who also had the job of looking after the rector's horses. One day the rector came across Ebenezer standing idle in a field beside the plough and team and asked why he wasn't working. Ebenezer said he was resting the horses.

"Well, my good man," said the rector, "Next time you come out bring your hook and while you are resting the horses you can busy you8rself trimming the hedge."

The following Sunday, when Ebenezer was on duty in church, the rector was most surprised to find on mounting the pulpit that it contained a knife and a bowl of potatoes. After the service he asked his church warden why on earth he had placed these curious objects there.

"Dew I kin trim a hidge tyme I'm restin' my hosses," said Ebenezer, "I reckon yew kin peel them spuds tyme yew're a'preachin' yar sermon."

RIGHT SPIRIT

A variety of gifts were bestowed on the rector of a Norfolk village church as he was moving on to pastures new. Among them was a bottle of choice cherries preserved in old brandy.

The rector wrote to say thank you to the donor, saying how much he appreciated this handsome gift....

"But I appreciate even more the spirit in which they were sent!"

Gert: "Orl yew read these days is how smokin' an' drinkin' are wholly bad fer yew..."

Florrie: "Only one thing for that my gal – give up readin'!"

PROUD BOAST

A man goes into confession and says to the priest: "Father, I'm 82 years old and married. I have four children and eleven grandchildren. Last night I went out and met two eighteen year old blondes. I made love to both of them. Twice."

The priest says: "Well, my son, when's the last time you were at confession?"

"I've never been to confession before – I'm Jewish"

"So why are you telling me?"

"Oh, I'm telling everyone."

STRONG BACKING

Old Jimmy went to the vicar and asked him to pray for Sally Grey. The vicar mentioned her in his prayers on the next two Sundays.

Before the service the following week Jimmy told him prayers were no longer necessary.

"Has the poor dear passed away or is she better?" asked the vicar.. "Oh, no" said Jimmy. "She won the 3.30 at Yarmouth larst Wednesday."

PLAY IT COOL

Patrick goes to confession and says to the priest: "Bless my Father for I have sinned. I have been with a loose woman."
The priest says: "Is that you, Patrick?"
"Yes, Father, it's me."
"Tell me, who was the woman you were with?"
"I cannot tell you, Father. I don't wish to ruin her reputation."
"Was it Teresa?"
"No, Father."
"Was it Mary?"
"No, Father."
"Was it Bernadette?"
"No, Father."
"Very well, Patrick, I can see you're not going to tell me. Go and say five Our Fathers and four Hail Marys."
Patrick goes back to his pew. His pal Tommy whispers to him: "So what happened?"
Patrick says: "It was OK. I got five Our Fathers, four Hail Marys and three damn good leads."

Gert: "I'm thinkin' o'standin' fer the parish cownsil."

Florrie: "Yis – but dew yew think they'll stand fer yew?"

A little bit o' Squit

The little old lady was spending her birthday as a patient in the Norfolk & Norwich University Hospital. Pride of place on her bedside locker went to a card with the message: "To my bewtiful wife."

"This one," the patient announced proudly to all her visitors, "wuz sent ter me by my husband. But the sorft ole fewl fergot ter sign his name!"

IT'S A SNIP

A vicar known for his lengthy sermons noticed a man get up and leave during the middle of his oration. The man returned just before the end of the service. Afterwards the vicar asked him where he had been.
"I went to get a haircut" came the reply.
"Why didn't you do that before the service?"
"Because," he said, "I didn't need one then."

SOUND REPLY

The vicar climbed into the pulpit to start his formal liturgy. He had a habit of tapping the microphone to make sure it was on.

This time there was no sound coming back, so he exclaimed…."There's something wrong with this microphone."

Thinking the vicar had started his liturgy the congregation replied obediently "And also with you."

WELCOME!

A bishop visited a village church and found a smaller than usual congregation.

"Did you tell them I was coming?" he asked the old verger.

"No, ole partner" he replied, "but news must he' got out somehow."

A little bit o' Squit

Many Norfolk people used to fix dates by seasonal occupations. For instance, when a new vicar asked a parishioner how long she'd been a widow, she replied: "Now, let me see…if he'd ha'lived till next muckspreadin', he'd a'bin dead ten year."

Gert: "She say she'll never marry a man what snore."

Florrie: "Well, she want ter be wholly careful how she find out."

A little bit o' Squit

Old Ezra was a bit unsteady on his feet as he left The Black Horse. He stumbled and fell, prompting a smart young woman passing by to rush to his aid.

"Are you all right? Have you got vertigo?"

"No, my bewty. Jist round the corner."

KEEP IT SIMPLE

The minister was visiting an elderly parishioner and agreed to pray with her that she might have better health.

As they knelt together on the floor he began: "Dear Lord, if it be your will, please restore Mrs Higgins to her former health."

He felt something tugging his sleeve.

"Excuse me" said the old lady, "Call me Mabel...He wunt know me by my married nearme."

Gert: "Yew'll never guess who I bumped intew at th'optishun's yisty."

Florrie: "Dunt tell me..... evrabody!"

➡Comeback Kings

Strangers, newcomers and even well-heeled locals who might consider themselves much smarter than the Norfolk yokels should beware native wit and wisdom. A slow and deliberate response can leave the sharpest inquisitor on the ropes.

Arrogance and sarcasm are met with the choicest answers. Take old Horry showing an American tourist around the village:

"Thass our chatch. Took nigh on twetty year ter build centuries ago....."

"Gee, I guess back home in Kentucky we could have built one in five."

"Thass our new school. Only took nine month ter build that......"

"Gee, I guess back home we could put up a school in six months."

They turn a corner where stands the village hall.

"Say, buddy, what's that building over there?"

"What, that one? Dunno, ole partner, that wunt there when I come ter work this mornin'..."

⌐

A Norfolk mawther went up to London to work in a big house where there were many other servants who laughed at her for being a "country cousin".

One day she came back from shopping and rang the doorbell for admittance. The footman let her in and remarked in a rather haughty voice: "Well, here's our little country cousin back safe and sound."

She gave him an old fashioned Norfolk look and replied: "There now, ent Lunnon a rare wunnerful plearce....all yew ha' got ter dew is push a button an' out pop a fewl!"

⌐

Then there was a Norfolk farmer in a surprisingly jovial mood after a bumper harvest. He thought he'd have a bit of fun with old Ben, supposed to be a few sticks short of a bundle.

"Now, Ben, take a wheelbarrow and a four-tined fork and empty the water out of the horse pond so I can fill it up again with fresh rainwater."

Old Ben duly wandered off to collect the wheelbarrow and fork from the other side of the farm. The farmer stood smirking as he passed. Then old Ben turned round…..

"Now, marster, afore I git on a'doin' that there pond, what dew yew want me ter dew wi' the water – spreed it or leave it in piles?"

Another winner in this department concerns a jolly chap from the BBC television documentary department asking about Lord Nelson's connections with a certain Norfolk village.

He saw old Billy sipping his half in the corner of the local and said with exaggerated bonhomie: "My good man, what can you tell me? You remember Nelson, don't you?"

"Yis," replied Billy as he slowly looked up. "But I still liked his father best."

I was caught out by a veteran villager during a wireless programme some years ago.

"Have you lived there all your life?" I asked in a perfectly reasonable manner.

Came the devastating reply: "No, not bluddy yit, I hent!"

My favourite Norfolk riposte came from Henry "Shrimp" Davies, Cromer lifeboat legend and twinkling mardler. He had been home from the sea as Cromer coxswain for over a decade by the time I moved to the town in 1988.

"Welcome to the coast, boy – and dunt go out there when the water's lumpy!"

We met regularly on the promenade for a Sunday morning chat. Shrimp mixed memories and character sketches with pithy comments on all kinds of topics. This is the priceless yarn I have dined out on many times.

He came up to me one morning and said: "We dunt harf git some rum'uns round here, dunt we?" he teased. I played the game and asked what on earth he meant.

"This chap come up ter me in Jetty Street th'uther day an' started slaggin' orff the plearce… 'Bloomin' Cromer – thass the backside o'Norfolk!' he growled."

So what did Shrimp say to that?

"I looked him strearte in the eye an' said: 'Oh, yes, an' are yew jist passin' through?'"

That inspired me to build up a collection of slick comebacks from folk supposed to be a bit slow on the uptake.

How do I get to Fakenham?
Well, I shunt start from here if I wuz yew.

Where does this road go to, my good man?
That dunt go nowhere – that stay here where thass wanted.

Why are the church bells ringing?
Cors somewun's a'pullin' the rope.

A little bit o' Squit

A Norfolk lad went on his first date. His father noticed he was carrying a lantern.
"What are yew doin' wi'that, boy? I dint tearke no lantern when I went a'courtin'."
"No," replied the boy, "an' jist look what yew come home with!"

A little bit o' Squit

The farmer and his wife were discussing how to celebrate their silver wedding anniversary.
"Shall I kill a chicken?" asked the wife.
The farmer replied: "Why blame a poor bird for something that happened twenty-five years ago?"

Do you have matins in your church?
No – we hev lino right up ter the altar.

Do you think the farmer could use me on the land?
No – they've got speshul stuff fer that nowadays.

How far apart shall I plant my potatoes?
Harf in yar garden – an' harf in mine.

Your potatoes are on the small side this year
Ah, well, I grow 'em ter fit my mouth, not yours.

Gert: "How dew I stand fer borrowin' a tenner?"

Florrie: "Yew dunt – yew git on yar knees!"

Can I trust you to keep a secret?
Cors yew kin – thass them I tell it to what carnt.

Are you in favour of progress?
Yis – long as nobody dunt change noffin'

Why on earth are you pulling that piece of string?
Well, dew yew come an' try pushin' it.

Is that river good for fish?
Reckon that must be – I carnt git enny ter leave it.

How would you like to be up there in that aeroplane?
Well, I shunt want ter be up there wi'out it.

Have you had your eyes checked?
No – they've allus bin blue.

How far do you reckon I am from Watton?
Oh, 'bowt the searme distance as me.

Are you going to old Jacob's funeral?
No – and I dunt reckon that miserable ole beggar'll come ter mine!

Sea Here Boy! Cromer lifeboat legend Henry "Shrimp" Davies had a twinkling sense of humour to go with his no-nonsense Norfolk style.

NORFOLK PROVERBS

The older I git, the better I useter be.

Thass allus best ter speak the truth – unless yew're a rare good liar.

"A box of pills, please. "Antibilious"? "No. Uncle is."

Half a loofah is better than no bath at all.

Empty vessels ....mean Horry hent stood his round agin.

Thass smart ter pick yar friends – but nut ter pieces.

Dunt believe evrathing yew hear – but repeat it jist ter be on the safe side.

Gert: "I hear they had a colleckshun for a man in Deirdre's orffice...?"

Florrie: "Yis – but they dint get enuff munny ter buy wun!"

Forgive yar enemies – but dunt fergit their names.

If yew keep yar mouth shut, yew'll never put yar foot in it.

People who live in glass houses…myte as well answer the doorbell.

Thass wholly nice ter dew noffin – and then have a good rest arterwards.

He who larf larst ….probably dint git the joke in the fust plearce.

Yew kin mearke many a false step by standin' still.

Gert: "Sorry I'm learte, ole partner. I sprained m'ankle."
Florrie: "Huh, nut anuther learme excuse!"

A little bit o' Squit

Little Troshing Rovers were playing Puckaterry Parva United in a Norfolk village football cup-tie. The referee came from Lower Dodman.

He called the two captains together before the kick-off and said: "Look, lads, afore this arternoon's over thass a gorn ter git wholly foggy. What dew yew say we play th'extra tyme first?"

Some men git what they deserve....others stay single!

Too menny cooks ....finish up on tellervishun.

Never put orff till termorrer what yew kin dew next week.

Allus hev one foot on the ground afore yew lift th'uther one up.

Look afore yew....ouch!

When the wind is in the east – that'll stay there till that shift!

A little bit o' Squit

A Norfolk farmer looked over the hedge to see the lad he had sent bird scaring stretched out and relaxing.

"You won't get far in this job if you don't buck up" he called.

"I know how far I got," came the reply, "cors I put a stick in where I left orff."

A trubble shared is .....all round the village in harf an hour.

People are wholly generous wi' what corst 'em noffin.

Stay safe on Bonfire Night ....stand well clear o'yarself.

If yew want breakfast in bed...dew yew sleep in the pantry.

Yew know yar kids are growin' up when they stop askin' yew where they come from – but wunt tell yew where they're a'gorn.

Patience is puttin' up wi' people yew'd rather put down.

Gert: "They dew say he hev got a brain like Einstein's."

Florrie: "What – dead since 1955?"

SQUIT VERDICTS

One of squit's strongest suits is a capacity for appealing to people of all types – even those who see the light, follow it and end up in God's Own Acre known as Norfolk. Some incomers, dubbed "furriners" by less-gracious locals who like a bit of healthy aggravation, are brought by a change of job or a new appointment which invariably spells promotion. (Bishops, Chief Constables, County Hall mandarins and head teachers spring to mind).

Many seek retirement pastures on or near a captivating coastline where they spent happy holidays. Then there's the returning native wondering why it isn't quite the same as when he left it just after the war.

We have to put up with a more cosmopolitan feel to the old place as development pressures intensify and Norfolk is "discovered", particularly around fashionable fleshpots like Burnham Market. Good for the economy, but not so hot for the traditional Norfolk character.

This is where squit really comes into its own as indigenous remnants dig deep, recall the Vikings and pretend to know very little about new-fangled ways introduced after Queen Victoria's funeral.

Their novelty value ensures some form of peaceful co-existence and a liberal use of squit leaves visitors and newcomers swifter to bless rather than to chide. Dark oaths soaked in broad dialect and accompanied by a throaty chuckle, saucy wink and confidential stoop tend to be taken as rich compliments, even in broad daylight.

I sought out a number of Norfolk luminaries, some of them nurtured in other ways in other places, to share their ideas of what squit might be. Their ready responses underlines the way it takes a grip on all sorts of folk at all levels of society. Here are their considered offerings:

THE BISHOP OF NORWICH
THE RT REV GRAHAM JAMES

I came to Norfolk from Cornwall, my native county. The Cornish have a reputation for being taciturn, contrary and suspicious of what they call emmetts (the Cornish word for ant which is applied frequently to the non-Cornish swarming all over the county).

Norfolk does different but I recognised some of the features. True Norfolkmen were not going to be impressed by this new bishop landing in their midst – and who could blame them?

In my first month or so I was on a visit to a parish in North Norfolk and got chatting to a true Norfolkman in the local pub. "Where do yew live?" he asked me. "In Norwich" I said, "right next to the Cathedral". "Norridge", he replied, "I went there wunce".

That, for me, is a perfect rejoinder. He tells you nothing about his feelings for Norwich, but also tells you everything. That's the secret of Norfolk squit – or so I think

Distance is different in Norfolk as well. I've only got to travel twenty miles from Norwich for an evening Confirmation to be asked by half a dozen people "Are yew goin' back to Norridge tonite?"

The best Norfolk story I've heard was told by Simon Broke, Chairman of our Board of Finance at a Diocesan Synod. He remembered an experience of one of my predecessors, Lancelot Fleming, many years ago.

Apparently after the bishop spoke at some great gathering one Norfolk churchwarden said to the other "Did you 'ear the bishop say that Windum wuz better 'an Norridge?"

"Did 'e say that? Windum wuz better'n Norridge?"

"Yes, I'm sure he said Windum wuz better'n Norridge."

"I can't believe it, Bishop of Norridge sayin' that Windum is better'n Norridge".

"I asked around, various other people who agreed that the Bishop had said that Windum was better'n Norridge".

Then they saw the Bishop himself, so they decided to ask him direct:

"Did you say that Windum was better'n Norridge?"

"No" said the Bishop. "I said that wisdom is better than knowledge".

Put in the hands of a Norfolkman, this New Testament is a dangerous thing!

A little bit o' Squit

Sales assistant to Norfolk housewife: "Madam, this cooker is very economical. It will pay for itself in no time at all."

Norfolk housewife: "Well, when that dew, jist yew hoss that 'round my place."

A little bit o' Squit

Lady teacher: "Consider this sentence – 'I don't have no fun at the weekend'. How should I correct this?"

Billy: "Git yarself a boyfriend."

Gert: "Dew yew believe in loyalty?"

Florrie: "Yis – when a woman reach th'age she like, she orter stick tew it!"

PROFESSOR PETER TRUDGILL

Internationally acclaimed expert in linguistics with deep Norfolk roots. President of FOND – Friends Of Norfolk Dialect

When you ask an academic linguistic what the word squit means to him, you are, I'm afraid, bound to get an academic answer.

I suppose squit means the same to me as it does to everyone else in Norfolk and Suffolk, although I have to say that it is by no means only an East Anglian word, being found in the local dialect as far away as Herefordshire – and you can't get much further away than that.

But I though the boy Keith might be interested in what I could find out about the origins of this word. It turns out, though, that the answer is rather indelicate, so I will try and find a form of words that will not bring maidenly blushes to the cheeks of Keith, or anyone else in Cromer for that matter.

Actually, the origins of squit are a little obscure, but the best guess that the world's collected lexicographers can come up with is that it is a form of the word squirt, with a loss of the consonant 't'. (Think of horse and hoss, burst and bust.) The same connection can be seen in the fact that a small person can be referred to contemptuously, in different parts of the country, as 'a little squirt' or 'a little squit'.

But in our meaning of 'nonsense', it makes more sense to compare the word to the rather disagreeable phrase the squits. Even Keith should be able to see the connection here with the original form of the word with an 'r'. And it should now be easy to work out, if you stop and think about it, why our ancestors should have started using a word derived from squirt to mean 'nonsense'. But please don't let this stop you using this, now harmless, word.

The meanings of words can change through time, and any linguist will tell you that the historical origins of a word may have nothing to do with its current meaning. (The original meaning of nice, for instance, was 'ignorant'!) Our word squit means what we know it means. Except that it, too, has changed a little in meaning in recent years.

Academic linguists will tell you that individual people cannot change the meaning of words all by themselves, even if Humpty Dumpty thought he could. But in this case they are wrong. Squit has increasingly acquired over the last decades the additional and very agreeable meaning of 'enjoyable nonsense'. And we all know who takes the credit (if that is the right word) for that....

Gert: "They dew reckun that Martha is a bit on the tight side...."

Florrie: "Tight? She sharpen har pencils over the fireplace so she wunt wearste wood!"

LORD ROBIN WALPOLE
OF MANNINGTON HALL

Of course I know what it is and so do you. But how do we explain it to others? Maybe by the end of this Bumper Book you will have the answer!

Some of you will be groaning "not another book on Norfolk Squit". I understand that the Cambridge University Library adds miles of books each year and the Trafalgar bi-centenary has produced yards more so another book on squit may be the straw that breaks the camel's back (or should it be the donkey's?)

I grew up with it, born and bred in Norfolk and there can be no doubt that my distinguished relatives Sir Robert Walpole, his brother Horatio (the first Lord Walpole) not to mention Nelson, all exchanged these remarks with their fellow countrymen often when in distant parts (well, in London anyway) and felt more at home.

We do enjoy the sly comment about our fellow worker. We all know the one described thus: "His hand don't reach the bottoms of his pockets". Somehow it's kinder than "mean old swine" but just as derisory.

Life often puzzles us; how often have we heard "Thas a rum'un," but it can't be easy for someone not brought up to it to understand "Thas a rum'un he hent done it – I thought he would ha' done thet by now."

Our accent causes problems. Imagine the new, foreign (well, Suffolk) farm foreman being told: "I hev some sex in my shud".... I know he means he's got some sacks in his shed but ....it could cause some trouble.

We all know there's a lot of squit talked about sport but sometimes that's short and sweet. "Lorst one ought" translated to "Norwich City lost another game one nil they should have won."

But there's logic too. Trying to pin down an employee (past retiring age) as to when he might retire (people like the Inland Revenue like to know these things), he said: "Time I feel alright I'll keep a'comin' (and he did!)

Then there were the two plumber brothers, one short, one tall. When I asked how they decided on the height of the new urinals fitted at the Mannington entrance (a British standard perhaps?) the reply was "Thas easy gov'nor, I dew the men and he dew the boys"!

I wish Keith all the best and long may his books continue to amuse and instruct us, keeping alive the old Norfolk ways and informing the world we still "du different".

HELEN McDERMOTT

Anglia Television personality

I come from Irish stock (slightly), so perhaps I'll be better off with o'squit. But there are similarities between the Norfolk people and the Irish.

On holiday in Ireland we were in a pub which had hundreds of bicycles outside. A local walked in and asked loudly: "Anyone own a bike?"

In a restaurant we sampled a bottle of red wine. For the first time in my life I said I didn't like the wine – I'm no connoisseur so it must have been bad. The Irish waiter replied: "Ah, to be sure, it's meant to taste like that"

So we drank it.

In another restaurant we asked the waiter about odd requests from diners. Apparently someone asked for "avocado with a pear".

On a countryside trip by horse and cart I asked the owner if his nag liked taking tourists for a ride. Naturally, I was expecting him to reply that we love tourist people and fresh air – but he solemnly replied: "I doubt it".

I've been in this lovely part of the world for over 25 years and received loads of lovely letters from viewers. One asked me to marry him or send a photo.

One sent a pair of knickers, declaring that every time I wore a brooch on the tele he'd know I was wearing the garments he sent. (Ever seen me wearing a brooch on TV?) Worst thing about it was that the knickers were about a size 30. I was sorely tempted to write back and ask for a smaller pair!

A little bit o' Squit
One Norfolk lad to another on seeing a well-powdered and painted woman go past: "Blarst, thass poor land what need orl that muckspreadin'!"

A little bit o' Squit
A Norfolk lad who had been promised a baby brother or sister for his birthday said to his mum: "If that dunt mearke yew tew big, I'd like a Shetland pony an'orl."

ED FOSS
Journalist with the Eastern Daily Press

High falutin philologists and linguists would have us believe the definition to be something of this nature: Informal, low-brow discourse presented in the comic form, for pleasure.

Those who participate in squit, however, will provide a very different definition, one which will invariably be long, drawn-out and, to be blunt, unnecessarily circuitous, while failing dismally to reach a conclusion. But one which will make you smile, either at the time or later, probably both.

Squit is a waste of time, in the same way that walking along a sunny beach arm in arm with a loved one is a waste of time.

Is it in the Oxford English Dictionary? Perhaps a campaign could be started – after all 'chav' and 'Yarco' have made it onto those esteemed pages.

Squit is what some of us do when we have forgotten what we are supposed to be doing – dull pastimes such as work, shopping, watching reality television, considering the weather in far too much depth and arguing with wives, husbands or lovers about the washing up.

It requires no education and gets us nowhere, but the trip itself is well worth it.

Just like cricket, squit is pointless but marvellous. One day a scientist will recommend a daily dose of squit as a cure-all, along with two glasses of red wine and an avocado.

PETER WILSON
Chief Executive of Norwich Theatre Royal

I used to produce the stage shows of a great American humorist called Garrison Keillor, whose false-folksy tales of Lake Wobegon became quite a cult in the 1980s.

Garrison's stories always began with "It has been a quiet week in Lake Wobegon" and then developed into outrageous and entirely credible tales of a small midWestern Lutheran community riven by depression and understatement – as in the man who, embarking on an adulterous evening, took with him a six-pack of beer "to dull the pleasure"!

A little bit o' Squit

Overheard in a Norfolk village shop:
Old lady: "Could I hev three pound o'pertaters, please."
Shopkeeper: "Do you want the large or small ones?"
Old lady: "Oh, I'll tearke the little'uns... them big'uns are tew heavy ter carry."

A little bit o' Squit

Old Frank was leading his mare and tumbril when an American tourist stopped his car to comment on the small size of the "wagon".
"Huh," said Frank, "that ent my wagon. I go back arter that. This is where I keep my 'bacca."

Or his story of the skipper who couldn't find a way of telling his clients that the boat was sinking "without sounding negative".

I loved Garrison's deep tranquil voice as he formed a complete picture of this depressive displaced Scandinavian community – whose occasional bouts of Swedish flu had exactly the same symptoms as Asian flu, except that just before you took to your bed you suffered a compulsion to clean the house – and began to understand how the kind of detail he gave us was a rapid sketch of the entire world in miniature.

That's the best of squit, as I understand it. You hear in a few sentences the rhythm of an entire community. Those of us who are lucky enough to have found homes in Norfolk are also fortunate in being surrounded by a tongue which Keith, Sid Kipper, the Nimmo Twins and Canon Ivan Bailey (among others) have treasured for the rest of us to savour.

My personal favourite – as opposed to the many that I've been told – came at Swaffham Market one Saturday morning. It seems to me to encompass an attitude to customer care that would leave any of our modern stores gasping.

We had guests for the weekend and I'd been sent to look for raspberries. One of the stalls had a couple of punnets and I asked to buy them. "Blast, I can't dew that" she said, "cors if I sell them ter yew I'd have nun left for nowun else."

You see the important thing here? Not to sell everything, but to satisfy everyone. Delicious.

Gert: "What dew yew mean yew're hevin' amnezier an' dejar-vew at the searme time?"

Florrie: "Well, I think I're forgotten this afore!"

SIR NICHOLAS BACON
OF RAVENINGHAM HALL

One of my favourite Norfolk yarns, probably dismissed by many as a load of old squit, concerns rabbit pies.

A small farmer in Norfolk decided to diversify. He thought "There's a rare lot o'rabbits round here, so I orter take advantage an' mearke them inter rabbit pies."

One of the many people who bought one every day said they were the best pies in the county.

This chap had to go away on business for about a year. When he came back he immediately made tracks for the farmer's rabbit pie. He is horrified to discover they weren't nearly as good as they had been originally.

He went to the farmer and said: "Woss a'gorn on? Them pies dunt fare as tasty as what they used to."

The farmer replied: "Well, them rabbits hed that myxomatosis, so there wunt ser many on'em about. I hed ter fill out them pies wi' hoss meat now we're got the tractor an' dunt use the hosses."

The chap says: "How much hoss meat d'yer reckon ter put in?"

"About fifta – fifta" said the farmer.

The chap looked rather puzzled, "What d'yew mean by fifta – fifta?"

"Oh, said the farmer, "one hoss, one rabbit."

Gert: "Did yar cousin's boy arnser that advert what say 'would yew like ter travel, meet people an' hev a bagful o' munny?'"

Florrie: "Yis – an' he mearke a wholly good bus conductor!"

Gert: "Is that trew yar Uncle Bert hed a rabbit's foot for thatty year?"

Florrie: "Yis – but his uther foot wuz quite normal."

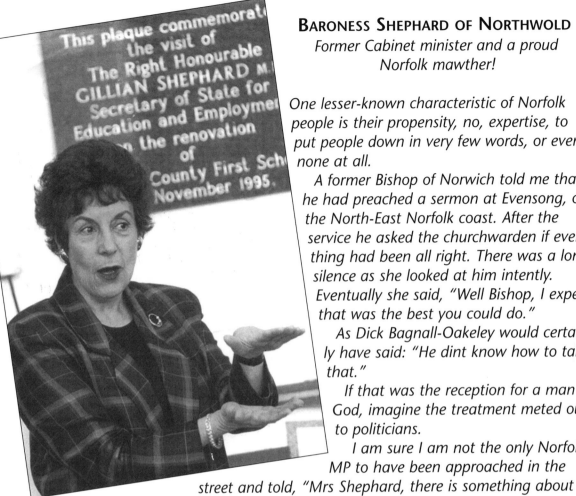

BARONESS SHEPHARD OF NORTHWOLD
Former Cabinet minister and a proud Norfolk mawther!

One lesser-known characteristic of Norfolk people is their propensity, no, expertise, to put people down in very few words, or even none at all.

A former Bishop of Norwich told me that he had preached a sermon at Evensong, on the North-East Norfolk coast. After the service he asked the churchwarden if everything had been all right. There was a long silence as she looked at him intently. Eventually she said, "Well Bishop, I expect that was the best you could do."

As Dick Bagnall-Oakeley would certainly have said: "He dint know how to take that."

If that was the reception for a man of God, imagine the treatment meted out to politicians.

I am sure I am not the only Norfolk MP to have been approached in the street and told, "Mrs Shephard, there is something about you I don't like. I can't put my finger on it, but that is so."

Or, there again, maybe I am.

All I can say is that examples abounded throughout my political career. One of the best, and most geographically authentic, since it took place in the Fens, was as follows. A man again approached me, in Downham Market, and said: "Mrs Shephard, I had thought I might give you a bag of onions, but they are rather dear at the moment."

They were 85p at the time.

Fortunately, I am from Norfolk too...

A little bit o' Squit

Charlie went to see a psychiatrist for several years. Eventually he was told he could cure his depression simply by going on holiday to the seaside.

A few weeks later the psychiatrist got a post card from Cromer bearing this message: "Hevin' a smashin' time. Why?"

SID KIPPER
*Modest folksinging megastar from
St Just-near-Trunch*

Well now, squit is...

Actually, that's not easy to say exactly what squit is, due to it being squit, if you take my meaning – or even if you don't. So I'll give you a for instants (since you're not offering to pay for it):

If I said St Just FC was the best football team in Norfolk, that'd be stupid. And if I said they were going to win the league next year, that'd be wishy thinking. Then again, if I said they were a clean-living, fine example of Norfolk manhood, that'd be an upright fib. But if I said St Just FC had been inducted by aliens, and competed on the Moon, then that'd just be squit – even though it might explain the way they play!

So, you see, squit is...

No, I'm no nearer, really. I'll go another way:

On the one hand they say Cyril Cockle is as good as his word, but that's not worth a lot, due to him talking squit all the time. On the other hand when old Eric Eel come in the pub they buy him a pint and ask him to tell them some of his old squit, so that's worth at least a pint.

And on the other hand the Eastern Daily Bread pay that Keith Skipper to write squit for them, and then they print it, so that must be worth loads.

So as you can see, squit is....

Let me try this:

You know what the squits are? Well, that's not the same as squit. So there you are – that's one thing I can say for certain. And I could go on, and say for certain all the other things what aren't squit. Like trolley-buses – they're not squit. Nor aren't hearing aids. Or mashed potato. And if I listed them all, then whatever was left, however improvable, would be squit. Mind you, that'd be a hell of a long list, so I haven't got the space to do that. Beetroot – that's another one.

You see, that's the thing with squit. You know it when you hear it, but you can't quite put your finger on it – and if you could you'd probably wish you hadn't.

So, finally, in confusion, squit is...

Look, I'm sorry, I can't rightly answer your question. But then again, when I look back through what I've writ, I may not have told you what squit is, but I reckon I just might have shown you!

Gert: "Why dew mountain climbers rope tharselves tergether?"

Florrie: "Ter stop the sensible wuns from gorn hoom!"

Squit & CULTURE

They may seem rather strange bedfellows, but I can offer emphatic proof that squit and culture can live comfortably together. For several years old friend Peter Whitbread, a professional actor for well over half a century, graced Norfolk stages with stirring evidence that he was completely rewriting the works of William Shakespeare in broad Norfolk. We will always be grateful for classics such as The Taming of the Coypu from a "cultural icon" who found it easy to surmise that the Bard could so easily have been born in Stratton-on-Strawless.

Many Press Gang shows, with me and a happy band of local entertainers banging the local drum, saw Peter in harmony with his dog on stage as the programme went from Bard to verse. Peter appeared as Launce and Jack as Crab (without an Equity card) in a memorable excerpt from Two Gentlemen of Verona. The poor old dog cowered under a verbal onslaught.

Jack was being groomed for even bigger roles, but Peter's untimely death towards the end of 2004 saw our canine chum retired to a boney fido dogs' home. The parts he could have savoured include Collieuranus; Hamlet, Prince of Denbark; Richard the Turd; The Comedy of Terriers; Dogberry, the constable in Mutt Ado About Nothing; As You Bite It; Julius Sieze'er and Falstaffordshire Terrier.

Peter's scholarship helped inspire a list of alterative titles Shakespeare would have selected had he written those wonderful plays in Norfolk. Match the local version with the genuine article – but no prompting or peeping through the curtains!

SHAKESPEARE'S ORIGINALS:

Much Ado About Nothing
The Merchant of Venice
Romeo and Juliet (or Anthony and
        Cleopatra, Or Troilus and Cressida)
The Comedy of Errors
Timon of Athens
The Merry Wives of Windsor
The Two Gentlemen of Verona
The Tempest
Hamlet
Measure for Measure
All's Well That Ends Well
The History Plays

NORFOLK TRANSLATIONS:

Lotter Squit Bowt Beggar Orl
Pedlar of Swaffham
Horry and Florry
–
Good Larf Fuller Mistearkes
Hossman of Acle
Happy Mawthers of Winfarthing
Cupple of Rum Clyents From Cromer
Bit Dark Over Will's Mother's
Roll-up
Dunnow Noffin Bowt Them Sentimeters
Ent Ser Bad if Nowun Git Hat
Boy Hinry, King Hinry, an' Wot Happened
        Afore and Arter Hinry

A little bit o' Squit

The old Norfolk roadman was busy when a posh car pulled up. The driver called out impatiently: "I say, you there, could you tell me the quickest way to Bury St Edmunds?"

"Yis," said the roadman, "dig a hole."

Now imagine some of your favourite quotations from Shakespeare being afforded the full Norfolk treatment:

From **Richard III**: - *"A dickey! A dickey! My kingdom for a dickey, ole partner!"* (A horse! a horse! my kingdom for a horse!).

From **Hamlet**: - *"Blarst me, poor ole Yorick! Wunner the best, he wuz, allus a good larf and full o' squit".* (Alas poor Yorick, I knew him Horatio; a fellow of infinite jest, of most excellent fancy).

From **Julius Caesar**: - *"Hey, my old bewties, just yew cop a lug this way fer a minnit. I hev cum ter stick poor ole Caesar six foot under, nut ter say wot a good ole boy he allus wuz!"* (Friends, Romans, countrymen, lend me your ears; I come to bury Ceasar, not to praise him).

From **Macbeth**: - *"Cleer orf, yew blarsted dawg!"* (Out, damned spot, out I say!).

From **Anthony and Cleopatra**: - *"Yew scratch my back, an' Iyll scratch yours!"* (I will praise any man that will praise me).

From **Henry IV, Part II**: - *"Ent that a rummun how he think he kin still dew orl them there things wot he ewsed to, but he carnt cors he's past it?"* (Is it not strange that desire should so many years outlive performance?).

From **Romeo and Juliet**: - *"Cheerio, ole bewty! That ryte upset me ter see yer go, but Iyll be bowt fast thing in th' mornin'!"* (Good night, good night! Parting is such sweet sorrow that I shall say good night till it be morrow).

From **The Tempest**: - *"Yew dunt owe nobody noffin when yew're dead an' gone"* (He that dies pays all debts)

From **Twelfth Night**:- *"Jist cors yew git on yar high hoss, that dunt meen we hatter cum in the stable wi' yer!"* (Dost thou think, because thou art virtuous, there shall be no more cakes and ale?)

Of course, Norfolk has long been a favourite haunt for cinema and television crews. From the grandeur of Blickling Hall to the rustic serenity of Heydon village green, the north of the county is rich territory for image-sellers.

Perhaps Dad's Army, on manoeuvres in Breckland, springs first to mind when television series are recalled. Many other production units are bound to head this way in years to come.

In compiling my list of the best 20 films projecting Norfolk as a centre of cultural excellence, I'm sorry to leave out such lavish musicals as Somerton Holiday, Oklaholkham and Singing in the Raynhams. There's no place for tantalising costume dramas like the Pride and the Paston, Beau Guist or the Admirable Croxton. And I've had to shove to one side wholesome westerns such as For A Few Ferrets More and Bad Day at North Creake.

However, those deemed worthy of top billing are indeed exceptional in calibre and likely to collect more awards in any roll of honour pieced together by film buffs. Here are my top 20 Norfolk delights.

One Flew Over the Turkey Shed

Morality tale set largely in the skies over Great Witchingham just before the festive season. A plump creature destined for the dinner plate plots a dramatic escape, only to have the stuffing knocked out of all the scheming by a self-seeking bantam. Sheer gobbledegook – but fowl play suspected.

Diss Family Robinson

Traditional fare. Family build a new home and a new life in inhospitable border country as they wait for the railway to bring prosperity. The Robinsons catch the gravy train, but it goes too fast for comfort. Telling flourish at the end as they pitch their tent on the banks of the Waveney.

Hingham High

The first spaghetti Eastern. A brooding stranger, claiming to be the reincarnation of Abraham Lincoln, rides into town for fresh provisions, only to discover it is early-closing day. He exacts revenge at a nearby supermarket by refusing to buy cactus on special offer. He avoids a lynch mob at the checkout counter and stays to become sheriff.

Citizen Cane

Epic story of a man with the fantastic idea of growing sugar on plantations at Limpenhoe and Lingwood and then processing it in a factory on the banks of the Yare at Cantley. He becomes a powerful newspaper tycoon instead when no-one will take the trouble to publish his adventures. Full of originality and invention, although it is a bizarre stretch of the imagination to call the factory foreman "Rosebud"

Carrowsell

Spectacular musical with songs as hot as mustard! Flashback sequences particularly memorable as old Jeremiah Colman, benevolent mill-owner, starts a school for children of his employees. "Father of my People" and "Look what's left on the plate!" Most hummable of many showstoppers.

> **Gert:** "What dew yew mean gal Ethel would mearke a good Guvn'r o' the Bank o' England?"
>
> **Florrie:** "Cors when she speak evrabody's interest rearte go down!"

A little bit o' Squit

A judge, in sentencing a notorious local offender, concluded by saying: "I hope that this is the last time you will appear before me."

"Why, my bewty," said the prisoner, "What are yew retirin'?"

A little bit o' Squit

The boy received a very bad school report. As his father pored over it, the lad asked casually: "Well, pop, what do you think is the real trouble with me... heredity or environment?"

COCKLESTALL HEROES

Defiant fishermen stand up to the mighty bureaucrats of Brussels and a hostile European press who dub them "The Shellfish Shockers". Wonderful scenes as the EEC "pirates" try to board the fishing boats by leaping off Cromer Pier, hounded in their efforts by the angry cast of the summer show. In the Ealing mould, but for home consumption only.

DR ACLE AND MR HEYDON

Whimsical treatment of the eternal battle between Good and Evil. A retired estate agent moves to a quiet corner of the countryside. His long-lost brother, an unscrupulous property developer, seeks permission to build over 200 houses at the bottom of the garden of this rural retreat. The brothers never meet...

THE MATLASKE FALCON

Private eye Sam Shovel digs up fresh clues in this novel treatment of the Dashiell Hamment crime melodrama. An archaeological dig unearths a priceless statuette and unleashes a trail of havoc across several villages. The L.A. background is more Lower Aylsham than Los Angeles, and this private eye is one of very few to accuse a suspect of talking "a load of old squit".

THE HOUND OF THE BASKETMEALS

Black Shuck, whose eerie presence has hounded the Norfolk coast for hundreds of years, finds a modern setting. He terrorises holiday pubs where customers are used to having food with their drinks. Strangely, he ignores the old-fashioned hostelries where a half of mild lasts all evening ... Slightly fanciful finale in the grand ring at Crufts, but enough authentic bits to satisfy Conan Doyle fans.

CLEY NOON

Classic confrontation between the hard-boiled native and the second-home stranger. The showdown over a plate of winkles in a birdwatchers' hide remains one of the most compelling in modern cinema. Haunting musical score and plenty of romantic interest as the locals plan big families in an effort to outnumber the incomers.

Gert: "What would yew like people ter say 'bowt yew in 100 years?"
Florrie: "Cor, blarst, she dew look well!"

BILL OF RIGHTS

When real horsepower ruled the furrows, the black-smith was a key figure in the farming community. The smithy often became the local "parliament" as characters met to put the world to rights. No doubt that was a common occurrence when Albert Sutton was at work in his North Norfolk village of Trunch.

A prime example of Norfolk humour coated in the delightful habit of running words into each other comes in this blacksmith's bill:

	s	d
Osforarfada	2	0
Afotheos	1	0
Ashuinonim	2	0
Anafechinonimagin	1	0
TOTAL	**6**	**0**

COYPU ECCLES

Norfolk's stirring answer to Crocodile Dundee – and note the neat cake connection! Our great white hunter leads the campaign to eradicate the area's most destructive pest. And when he's finished with speeding boats on the Broads, he turns to the coypu. Of course, being successful makes him another statistic on the jobless front, but he's ready for fresh challenges. Stand by for Grey Squirrel Nutloaf next year.

PAINT YOUR HONEYCART

Voted "Best Musical Before Going on the Mains", it enjoyed record runs in the old Forehoe and Henstead and Mitford and Launditch Rural District Council areas. The film is mostly set during the Californian Gold Rush before it spilled over into Hemsby and Winterton. It relies less on plot than out-standing numbers like "I Was Born Under a Gooseberry Bush". When it first hit the screens, patrons were asked to bring ten small squares of newspaper to the cinema to hang on a nail on the adjoining seat.

THE CANARY HAS LANDED

The one Jack Higgins forgot to write! This ripping yarn features enemy aliens from Suffolk infiltrating a Norfolk village in the hope of kidnapping Norwich City's star striker just days before the F. A. Cup Final at Wembley. Rather silly plot, as the Canaries were knocked out in round four. Cheerful romp for all that and Ipswich Town go on the lift the trophy.

Gert: "What dew yew mean he play second world war golf?"

Florrie: "Yew know – out in 39 and back in 45."

A little bit o' Squit

A motorist lost his way in rural Norfolk. He stopped to talk to a rustic leaning on a gate.

"Where does this road lead to, my good man?"

"Well, ole partner," came the reply. "One end lead ter my house, an' th'uther end go straight on."

CAISTERBLANCA

You must remember this…an affectionate salute to the changing face of the seaside scene as time goes by. Marvellous final scene where an old fisherman casts his nets – and his soul – into an unknown future and picks up a creature at the bottom of his boat, "The Boy John". He smiles as the sun sets and the water laps at his feet: "Here's looking at you, squid!"

THE GODWICKFATHER

Heartfelt nod towards the Norfolk Rafia, a group of cottage industry pioneers near Tittleshall. Inspired in part by "Silas Marner", the main character Matt Table is wrongly accused of stealing ideas from a rival community the other side of Fakenham. A looms showdown…..

YAXHAM DOODLE DANDY

Oscar-laden musical with deft patriotic backdrops. A chicken farmer goes into vaudeville and waves the flag for free-range eggs. Rather unpromising material stitched together in thrilling fashion as our buskin-clad hero struts magnetically across the rural stage.

ICE COLD IN ALBY

Family adventure set in the harsh winter of 1947. As the snow piles up, and the cupboards get barer, men and boys from the small villages battle across fields to get to the bakery for life-saving stocks. The bread becomes the obvious central symbol for wholesome country life, but the story is beautifully shot in black and white. Mostly white.

SCROBY DICK

Disney magic with a Norfolk flavour. A friendly white whale takes up residence just off Great Yarmouth and soon proves to be a big tourist attraction. He calls to the creatures in "The Kingdom of the Sea" on the Golden Mile to rebel and return to the wild. They demand half of the summer season's takings instead. Delightful satire on the holiday trade.

NORTH BY NORTH WALSHAM

The only film Alfred Hitchcock considered worth of a Norfolk setting. A computer salesman from Thetford is mistaken for a spy, and enemy agents left over from "The Canary has Landed" try to kill him. Chase sequence along the Southern Bypass is exciting, but the real drama unfolds when the salesman is run to ground by a crop-spraying tandem. Difficult to work out which side most of the characters are on, although Trunch W.I.'s rendition of "Jerusalem" puts them beyond the pale.

Bard Idea! *– Peter Whitbread, professional actor for well over half a century, often claimed William Shakespeare was born in Norfolk… at Stratton-on-Strawless.*

THE FRANSHAM CONNECTION

Cold War thriller in which all the players wear enigmatic smiles and knitted gloves. The "enemy" put a tail on everyone except the chap who has the Watercress File. Beautiful double-agents are either "Sinkers" or "Swimmers", according to their prowess in making good Norfolk dumplings, but they all end up in a right old stew. Rather dated, but the credits coming out of a bicycle pump still draw gasps of appreciation.

Gert: "Dew yar vet give penshuners discount?"

Florrie: "Yis – if yar dawg's over 65."

What's in a NAME?

I have long regarded every signpost on my Norfolk safaris as a juicy challenge. Indeed, it's a splendid game for all the family to come up with bright ideas as to how certain places might have got their names.

True derivations can be fascinating – for example Ashmanhaugh means "the pirates enclosure" and Bawsey "Gadfly island" – but it's much more fun to invent your own. Let's start with the county itself.

There are strong rumours that in the old days the people could be rather suspicious of strangers and, just occasionally, territorially minded. Newcomers from other parts of the country were even warned not to head this way in the first place. "Why not?" they would ask. "What's wrong with the Iceni?". Back came the answer – "They gnaw folk", although some early scholars of linguistics suggested it might have been "They ignore folk". Either way, the county became known as Norfolk and explains why it was so sparsely populated for so long.

Another school of thought gaining support is that the county was so named in the days before hosepipe bans and drought warnings when water levels were extremely high – "Noah folk". This theory was strongly backed by B Knyvett Wilson in his book Norfolk Tales and Memories, first published in 1930: "Some misguided people think 'Norfolk' is merely a shortening of 'North folk', but this is entirely wrong. The real derivation is 'Noah-folk', showing that we are all descended in a direct line from the great navigator and explorer.

"That this is so is patent from Noah's conversation with his son Japheth during an anxious moment in the Ark (I am not for the moment able to lay my hands on the reference). 'Jaaphet' he said, 'Ha, that mucky old dow come back yit?' to which Japheth replied 'Noo, faather, that ha'ent, not yit that ha'ent'. No-one could want better proof of our descent than that."

Sounds convincing enough to me. As does this explanation for the naming of Hindolveston:

When Norfolk was first invaded by men from the North, a dastardly Dane called Hindley the Horrible settled in a village somewhere near Fakenham. On seeing the locals in their customary garb, he felt they looked rather uncivilised…a rude smock

A little bit o' Squit

An old Norfolk farmer had electricity installed in his house for the first time after coming into some money.

"Thass wholly good," he told a friend. "I jist switch the light on' an' then I hev no trubble findin' the matches fer my candles."

made of assorted animal skins, a rabbit-skin cap on the head, the skin of a little fox in front of the body a little bear behind. He ordered the women to knit knee-length woolly vests which he ordered everyone to wear.

So, whenever people saw him approaching, up went the warning cry: "HINDLEY! VEST ON!" and that's how the village got its name.

Of course, there are several possible derivations for places with a charming name – like Stratton Strawless. I favour this one because it sounds the most likely:

A rambling club based in Norwich about three centuries ago decided to head towards the North Norfolk coast for a day out, but they weren't really sure how to get there because there were no maps or signposts. All the buses, charabancs, stages coaches and trains had been booked for Yarmouth. Well, it was a Bank Holiday, the 12th that year.

So that's why they were walking with coypu sandwiches, bottles of mead and wide-brimmed hats with dangling corks to guard against droppings from the Great Bustard flying overhead. They'd gone about seven miles north of Norwich after fighting off footpads and highwaymen on heathland near St Faith's, just past the airport, but couldn't find the sea anywhere.

Then, by a quirk of fate, they spied an ancient hedgetrimmer on the verge – on the verge of what it wasn't quite clear, but he did have half a smile on his face. In fact, he was also on the verge of trimming another hedge because that's what he did for a living after joining the Youth Opportunities Scheme in 1581 and he didn't want to go to Yarmouth.

One of the walkers sauntered over and gave him the seal of the day: "Good morrow, my good man, and what a fine job thou art doing for the environment. Tis a great pity there are not a few more like you about".

The old man winced: "Enough, you patronising city twerp! Just tell me what you want and move along before I trim your verge for you."

The rambler retorted: "Well, sire, we're trying to find our way to the North Norfolk coast before it falls prey to those who will exploit it for grubby commercial purposes."

The old man pointed a gnarled finger covered in bandages to a rough path across scrubland. The ramblers sallied forth. "Wonder where we are?" said one as they turned to see the old man waving his hook and calling to them.... . "Straight on, Strollers!".

Gert: "Dew yar ole man hev a war record?"

Florrie: "Yis – I think thass by Vera Lynn."

It hardly takes a giant leap of imagination to work out how this fine village got its name over 300 years ago on that fateful Bank Holiday.

Try the rest of these suggestions for size – and join in the fun as you travel around the county:

Ashill – scene of Norfolk's most famous smoking concerts in the early part of this century before they transferred to Hackford.

Aylsham – named after the first hypochondriac to be diagnosed locally in the National Health Service. He recuperated at Feltwell.

Barney – a rustic Mardi Gras where tempers could flare, especially if the "Best-Dressed Mawkin" contest was won by an outsider.

Barton Bendish – Uri Geller once had a holiday home in this small settlement, where you could find a sudden fork in the road.

Bawdeswell – comes from the cry of residents who ran bed-and-breakfast establishments in Chaucer's time as pilgrims approached ... "Come ye and reste awhile – four groats wille afforde ye bord as well!"

Belton – traditional call of Norfolk wife to husband dressing in haste. This followed a series of embarrassing incidents involving a mediaeval swineherd who took a short cut past the lady of the manner's summerhouse.

Bintree – resulted from the old country custom of tying a dustbin to a sycamore tree on Midsummer's Eve to ward off evil spirits. Fell into disuse after complaints about scattered rubbish.

Bircham – last outpost of corporal punishment in the county. The head of the village school came from Waxham, taking over from the notorious sisters whose cruel reign ended in 1865. They came from Frettenham and Lopham.

Gert: "Woss yar new bearby nephew called?"

Florrie: "Dunno – carnt unnerstand a word he say."

A little bit o' Squit

Village cricketer: "Howzat?"
Village umpire: "I wunt a'lookin'.
But if he dew it agin, he's owt!"

A little bit o' Squit

Teacher: "Tommy, name five things
that contain milk."
Tommy: "Butter, cheese... and
three cows."

Brancaster – before the enclosure of land in 1572, a miller at this coastal settlement "hurleth sifted huskes of Corne for pleasing the Harveste gods". The ritual ended when it snowed in August, 1569, but the bran caster is still remembered for his productive years.

Burnham Overy – originally "Burnham All Overy", referring to the wicked practice of incinerating awkward Britons by Roman conquerors.

Burston – home of the first pay-as-you-leave public convenience in the Diss area. The penny dropped elsewhere, including Puddledock and Riddlesworth.

Carbrooke – settlement strangely named after excuse for lateness proffered by Iceni taxi-driver to an angry Queen Boadicea.

Castle Acre – Royal Dentist's local headquarters. Ordinary mortals took their chances at Pulham Market or Gasthorpe.

Corpusty – in memory of much-loved local baker whose meat pies were famous for miles. Satisfied customers would lick their lips and exclaim: "Cor! Pasty"… and the name has been doing the rounds ever since.

Dereham – regular complaint to butcher, especially during the reign of Elizabeth I. Usual reply, laced with Norfolk wit, was to "go yew an' join Will Shakespeare when he ask for a cheap side!"

Gert: "That bor Hinry tork a lot o' ole squit, dunt he?"

Florrie: "Yis – orl his yarns hev gone way parst their tell-by date!"

Diss – originally one of a famous pair in south Norfolk. The other community, ling since disappeared, was called Datt.

⌐∿∿⌐

Ditchingham – this village name derived from a social meeting place where former sweethearts met to divide any spoils they might have collected together. A shrewd local opened an ale-house where those parting company could enjoy a civilised farewell with background music. "The Last Dance Saloon" once rivalled Gretna Green in the popularity stakes.

⌐◆⌐

Edgefield – village with a cricket ground where batsmen had all the luck. There were no boundaries at Runhall, and batsmen had to buy a round if they made a duck at Daffy Green. (See W G Grease's "Norfolk Cricket Curiosities", published by Bindertwine Books, 1911.)

⌐∿∿⌐

Egmere – famous for being described by a passing culinary expert as "not so much a hamlet – more a tasty omelette!"

⌐◆⌐

Elsing – rather fanciful notion that this parish was named after the famous Spanish tenor, although there is no record of his giving a concert in the village hall.

⌐∿∿⌐

Gert: "Dew yew reckun there's a lot o'diffrunce atwin husbands?"

Florrie: "Nut much – yew myte as well keep the fust wun!"

A little bit o' Squit

Two old Norfolk boys watched a hearse roll slowly by. As it disappeared into the distance one asked: "Who died, then?"
    "Him in the box, I reckun" said the other.
    "Yis," mused the first, "driver looked all right."

Fakenham – birthplace of the county's most notorious forgers, the Picasso Brothers.

Felmingham – location of the first BBC television wildlife crew to penetrate the more rural parts of Norfolk. "We were really looking for David Attleborough" said a spokesman.

Great Cressingham – another connection with The Great Summer Game. This village was named after a compliment to Ingham Cricket Club's travelling tea ladies for their outstanding sandwiches.

Great Snoring – possibly the birthplace of Rip Van Winkle, although there are bigger dormitories in the county.

Great Moulton – so called after a 16th century tragedy in this turkey-rearing area when a freak storm resulted in the complete loss of feathers by the whole flock. Members of a local coven were blamed, with locals muttering: "They've been witching 'em!"

Halvergate – named by a Norwich City Football club chairman, who, when asked what the crowd was like at Carrow Road that afternoon, replied: "Hell of a gate!"

Hickling – catcalls in a Broadland village, usually aimed at coracle users going too fast. (Not to be confused with "Hick – Lyng", the way in which a student from that village introduced himself on "University Challenge".)

Gert: "Did yew enjoy the panto, then?"

Florrie: "Nut reely – that Aladdin rubbed me up the wrong way."

PANTO PAIR

"You can always tell a Norfolk man......"
"Ah, but yew carnt tell 'im much!"

A bit of saucy backchat as Keith Skipper tries to string Nora Batty along with a sensuous and witty line. She resisted the charms of this Norfolk Compo throughout the 1982-83 pantomime production of Mother Goose at Norwich Theatre Royal.

Hockering – predictably from "Hock a ring", a nineteenth century pawnshop on the outskirts of the village.

Holt – used to be an army garrison town, taking its name from the traditional sentry's challenge during the Great Gresham Mutiny of 1827.

Howe – was an Indian reservation near the coypu's happy hunting ground. Big Chief Little Plumstead led the braves.

Lessingham – a delightful example of Norfolk whimsy. The village earned its name from a declaration made by tipsy carol singers.

Limpenhoe – here was formed the first agricultural commune for injured workers just after the Napoleonic Wars. Main benefactor was the Rev William Spooner, in whose honour the second commune was wet up at Spooner Row.

Melton Constable – long before it became the "Crewe of Norfolk" on the railway map, this was a notorious location for police passing-out parades in August.

115

Norton Subcourse – in the early part of this century a certain Davy Jones joined the Navy and embarked on a series of lectures on underseas warfare. He failed the examination with the lowest possible mark and was dismissed from the service. He retired to Norfolk and settled in "Nought On Sub Course".

Old Buckenham – the county's first Country and Western music centre with rodeo riding for the over 80s was set up here.

Paston – a famous burial place where priests carried out their duties to the letter.

Poringland – derived from its location at the heart of the East Anglian rain belt. Other heavy falls at Booton and the Raynhams.

Pulham St Mary – this name resulted from encouragement given to a local bell-ringer canonised in 1324AD. She was a milkmaid for many years.

Reedham – emerged at about the same time as Belton, inspired by an old-fashioned cry from spouse flinging bills across the breakfast table. The customary reply echoed the qualities of other villages, most notably Binham and Banham.

Repps – Norfolk's first college for commercial travellers was built here. It became Repps-with-Bastwick after the bad fire of 1921 when a bedside lamp exploded.

Saxlingham Nethergate – named after a memorable reply from a farmer asked by his workers what they should do with items collected from the barn…. "Sacks? Sling 'em near the gate!"

Scole – site of the earliest known educational establishment in the county, originally spelt Skool.

Gert: "I hear poor ole Mabel hev got a strained wrist."

Florrie: "Reckun she wuz born like that – tryin' ter hang on fer the weddin'!"

Seething – once inhabited by a tribe at loggerheads with everyone. They were sorted out by Big Chief Little Plumstead and his braves from Howe at the battle of Hot and Cold Running Water.

Shelfanger – first do-it-yourself evening classes held here. Wood Dalling and Hindringham (a course in civil disobedience) also very popular4.

Sloley – quite simply, the settlement named in honour of the true Norfolk way of life.

Stoke Holy Cross – in old days when trains used to stop at the village the fireman on the steam engine was most annoyed at being ordered to stoke the boiler when he had been looking forward to a good rest. The guard went along the platform shouting to boarding and alighting passengers: "Hurry up everyone …stoker's wholly crorss!". This was eventually accepted as the name of the station, although slightly corrupted on later years.

Three Holes – the impecunious village cricket club could afford only three stumps, later sold to provide a bat. The three holes remain to this day as a salute to pioneering sportsmen.

Trimingham – named in honour of National Toenail Cutting Day. Not to be confused with Crimplesham and National Hairdressing Week or Clippesby and the Annual Hedgegrowers' Convention.

Tuttington – people liable to make mistakes never settled here.

Wymondham – derived from the old custom whereby residents greeted strangers in their own special way – punching them in the stomach. If they recovered they would head for Downham in the hope of more civilised treatment.

Gert: "I think my old man is strayin' in his mind."

Florrie: "I shunt wurry – he carnt go far."

Squit Lives!

It has been a sheer delight to be at the heart of the squit survival campaign for well over two decades, drawing full houses in village, town and city with a potent mixture of home-spun humour, readings and songs.

The great team adventure started in the summer of 1984 in the Pavilion Theatre on Cromer Pier, home of the country's last authentic end-of-the-pier show. Dick Condon, one of the most inspirational characters I have ever met, convinced me squit would be a good traveller after that show attracted a sell-out audience. Dick had waved his Irish magician's wand three years earlier to turn me into a Norfolk "Compo" alongside the redoubtable Nora Batty (Kathy Staff) in the Mother Goose pantomime at Norwich Theatre Royal, a pleasure destined to reawaken my dramatic instincts.

I played several parts with Rackheath Players in the 1970s, thanks mostly to the encouragement of friend and colleague Ted Bell, Eastern Daily Press sports editor and a leading light with the local group. I also took the role of chairman for old-time music hall productions and that experience proved very handy in linking items on fresh entertainment rounds.

My travelling troubadours came under the Eastern Daily Press umbrella at the start of a busy 1996 season and we've been known as the Press Gang ever since. We have raised thousands of pounds for village halls, churches, schools and other

A little bit o' Squit

A Norfolk farm foreman paid a call on one of his workmen.

"Jimmy, I believe you lost two days last week."

"I know," said Jimmy, "I'm a gorn ter mearke that up Saturday arternoon."

A little bit o' Squit

Jacob came up with a perfect idea to cut his electricity bill:

"Thass easy. I only plug in the electric clock when I want ter know the time."

vital local facilities. We've raised a few thousand laughs as well to underline the sheer joy of live resistance in an era of push-button entertainment. It is the unashamedly old-fashioned flavour of Press Gang concerts that attracts big audiences and regular bouquets, especially in rural parts where the village social used to be at the heart of local life.

We simply go on the stage and entertain. People who might not have been in their village hall or community centre for years have told us how much it reminded them of home-made enterprises both before and after the last war. I know exactly what they mean after being weaned on such delights in my mid-Norfolk parish home of Beeston.

A Nissen hut on the old aerodrome was our palace of varieties. I heard wonderful echoes many times since we hit the road with our Norfolk offerings. Yes, there's a lot of nostalgia in the air, but it goes deeper than that. We see plenty of newcomers alongside the natives in our audiences – and I reckon we ought to take some credit for helping to forge a new community bond across the area.

We have been invited to take part in several local festivals, including Hunstanton, Dereham, Gorleston and Downham Market. We have appeared on city stages at Norwich Theatre Royal, the Playhouse and the Maddermarket. We have gone "up market" with a show at one of the county's best-loved stately homes. The Grand Saloon at Wolterton Hall, with its magnificent tapestries and beautiful views of the lake and park, makes a perfect setting for squit, wit and plenty more.

Wolterton Hall was also the venue for highly successful Aristosquits concerts I organised and compered to encourage the great and the good of the county to show off their party pieces in aid of the EDP We Care Appeal. A similar idea lured many of my fellow deputy lieutenants of Norfolk on to the Wolterton stage to "do a turn" for the same splendid cause so close to Press Gang hearts in recent times.

Squit, clearly, has many miles to go in the 21st century. Hopes are high that a new generation of local entertainers will take over when the Press Gang hang up their joke books. I asked some of my old friends and colleagues, many of whom have shared laughs with me since the 1980s, to pass on favourite yarns or reflections. Here are their offerings from the heart of Norfolk.

Gert: "That allus worry me things myte never git back ter normal."

Florrie: "Oh, ah...well, that allus worry me they alriddy hev!"

MIK GODFREY
Bard of Bodham and Norfolk bus driver

I hed two ole Norfolk mawthers a'sittin' behind me on the bus th'uther week. One onnem say ter th'uther: "I wuz sorry ter hear abowt yar Harbert. That wuz sudden, wunt it?"

Th'uther one, she say: "Yis, that wuz on the Sunday mornin'. I called him at seven o'clock an' he say he'll be gittin' up in a minnit. At har'past nine he still hent got up so I went up ter call him agin an' found he'd passed away.

"But there y'are," she say, "if he'd a'got up when I called him the fust time, he'd still be alive now."

GREG POWLES
Broadcaster and actor

Henry was a delivery driver for a builder's firm. After a busy week he was dog-tired so he pulled into Pretty Corner car park near Sheringham for a little lunchtime snooze.

No sooner had he fallen asleep in the van when there was a loud knock on the window beside his head. A middle-aged man leaned in and said: "Sorry, my ole bewty, but hev yew got the time on yer?" Henry looked at his watch with a sigh and said: "Thass ten ter one."

Henry closed his eyes again but had barely drifted off to sleep when there was another loud knock on the window. A tall lady opened the door and said: "I'm sorry to trouble you but do you have the time?" Henry rolled his eyes and replied: "Almost one o'clock."

Sick of the disturbances, Henry took a sheet of paper and wrote in big letters "I DO NOT KNOW WHAT THE TIME IS" and placed it in the windscreen.

Satisfied, he once again put his head down for some shut-eye, only to once again be disturbed by a knock at the window.

He opened the door to hear a young man say... "Thass jist arter ten parst one, mate."

PAT "MANGOLDGRINDER" MAITLAND
retired driving instructor

Young Billy and his very posh friend George were invited to a birthday party. Sitting at the end of the table meant they were last when the lady came with two pieces of cake.

Billy grabbed the biggest piece. "That was very rude" said George.

"What would yew ha'done if she'd come ter yew fust?" asked Billy.

His posh friend replied: "Well, I would have taken the small piece."

Billy came back as quick as a flash: "Thass what yew hev got – so what are yew wingeing abowt?"

Billy was walking up and down outside Heathrow Airport.
The security guard said: "Can I help you, sir?"

"Dunt rightly know," said Billy. "My brother is comin' hoom from Canada terday. He're bin away fer thatty year."

"That's nice," said the security guard. "Will you recognise him?"

"Never thowt 'bowt that," said Billy.

"Will he recognise you?" said the guard.

"That he will – I hent bin nowhere."

COLIN BURLEIGH
Toff of Toftwood and musician of note

A farmer needed to have one of his cows serviced. As he didn't own a bull it was suggested the local vet might be of use in providing artificial insemination. He duly rang the vet who made an appointment to call the following day.

He arrived next morning, splendidly attired, as he was on his way to a funeral after performing his duties. The farmer met him at the gate.

"Come yew alonger me, bor" said the farmer. "She's a'waitin' in the barn an' wunt be no trubble. She's nice an' quiet."

The vet followed him and prepared to do his job. The cow lashed out with one of its back legs and kicked him.

"I thought you said she is nice and quiet" said the vet.

The farmer replied: "Reckun yew're frightened har, bor. I bet she hent sin a bull wi' a bowler hat on afore!!"

A little bit o' Squit

Conjuror to Norfolk yokel: "Now, sir, would you be surprised if I fetched a rabbit out of your pocket?"

Yokel: "That I would anorl, ole partner."

Conjuror: "But why would you be so surprised?"

Yokel: "Cors I got a ferret in there."

DAVID "MUCK CARTER" LAMBERT,
Norfolk comedian and inspiration for all squit merchants

Grandma and Grandpa won a holiday in a competition. It was a fly-drive trip to the USA. When they picked up the car Grandpa asked the man at the garage to check the petrol.

"Over here, we don't call it petrol, we call it gas."

Grandma – "Wha' he say?"

Grandpa – "He say over here they don't call it petrol, they call it gas."

Grandma – "Oooooh."

Grandpa asked the man if he'd just lift the bonnet and look at the battery.

"Over here, we don't call it the bonnet, we call it the hood."

Grandma – "Wha' he say?"

Grandpa – "Over here they don't call it the bonnet, they call it the hood."

Grandma – "Oooooh."

The man asked: "What part of England are you good folks from?"

"We come from Attleborough, a small town in Norfolk" said Grandpa.

"Well, I'll be darned. When I was in England I was stationed at Mildenhall and I went out with a Norfolk girl. Do you know that was the worst sexual experience in my goddam life!"

Grandma – "Wha' he say?"

Grandpa – "He say he's met yew afore."

⌁⌁⌁

Grandpa went to Norwich and bought himself a brand new pair of brown boots. Grandma pretended not to notice as he paraded around the house. Later, upstairs in the bedroom he took all his clothes of – except for the brown boots.

"Dunt yew notice ennything?" said Grandpa.

She replied: "Only the searme ole things a'dinglin' an' a'danglin'."

"They are not a'dinglin' an' a'danglin'. They are pointin'. Pointin' at my new boots."

"Pity yew dint buy yarself a hat."

Gert: "Yew'll larn ter appreshiate yar ole man in time."

Florrie: "Thass a pity I hent got that sort o'time."

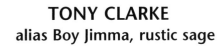

TONY CLARKE
alias Boy Jimma, rustic sage

Charlie, the landlord of Jimma's village pub, had a very bad habit. Whatever story of misfortune you told him he could always top it with his favourite phrase: "Mighta Bin Wuss."

One day Jimma thought up a brilliant story to defeat old Charlie.

"Dew yew know what?" he asked the landlord. "I went hoom larst night an' went upstairs an' see my missus in bed longer our neighbour. Dew yew know what I done?

"I went back downstairs, got my ole twelve-bore orff the wall, loaded that up an' put one shot inter har an' one inter him an' killed 'em both. What d'yer think o'that?"

"Mighta Bin Wuss" said Charlie. "Dew yew'd ha' come the night afore yew'd ha' shot me!"

ELIZABETH AUSTRIN
Gal Liza, dialect enthusiast

Us Norfolk folk are known for not using more words than is needed. Picture the scene – a busy doctor's surgery, receptionist at the desk, computer screen busy.

Enter a very elderly couple. Shuffling towards the desk, the little lady says: "Thass our feet."

What a good job there was a Norfolk mawther standing there ready to guide the couple to the chiropodist's room. No other words needed.

Gert: "Is that trew only good gals keep diaries?"

Florrie: "Yis – the bad 'uns dunt hev time!"

SHEILAH OLLEY
Norfolk Fairy – and schoolteacher

Billy's old mate was feeling a bit down in the dumps cors he "wunt gittin' nowhere wi' the gals."

Billy said: "Yew want ter dew what I dew. When I walk along the prom I put a tater down my trunks an' that usually work a treat."
So his mate thought: "I know, I'll git a sugar beet an' put that in my trunks."
So he got the biggest sugar beet he could find and he went walking up and down the prom.
Billy came along and said: "How yer gettin' on?"
His mate said: "Well, them gals still ent tearkin' no notice."
Billy said: "Well, if I wuz yew I'd put it down the front."

Billy's wife met an old friend. She said: "How yer gittin' on? Larst time I say yer wuz at the car boot sale."
Her friend replied: "Yis, an' dew yew know, I bought a bran' new toilet brush an' that wuz only 50p."
Billy's wife said: "How are yew gittin' on wi' that?"
"Oh," she said, "I think thass brilliant an' I'm gittin' on really well wi' it.
"But my Bert, he're gone back ter usin' pearper."

PAT NEARNEY
The Norfolk Nut and pantomime expert

This old Norfolk boy was a deep sea diver. One day he surfaced and it was obvious he had found something important.
Ripping off his mask he said: "Yew ent gorn ter believe this, but I're found the Titanic. Jist think, thass bin down there since 1912. An' I'll tell yew suffin' else...
"The swimmin' pool's still full."

Billy went down the pub. He told them all he'd just bought a DVD recorder.
"But you're on the dole. How can you afford that?"
Billy replied: "I sold the telly ter my next door neighbour."

124

KEITH LOADS
Regular comedian at the Thursford Christmas Spectacular

Old George's wife had died. He called the undertaker who asked when the funeral would be.

"Termorrer week" said George.

"Tomorrow week?" exclaimed the undertaker. "That's about ten days. Any reason for that?"

"Well, thass like this here, marster. We're bin married 47 year, an' when we wuz a'courtin' we allus said if we ever got married we'd have a quiet week on our own.

"This is the only chance I hev had, so I'm gorn ter hev it now."

Before she died, old George's wife said to him: "If yew ever git married agin, I'll scrap my way outer the ground an' haunt yer."

A year or two after she died, George did get married again. Someone said to him: "Aren't you worried by what she said?"

"Blarst, no," said George. "I buried har fearce down, so the more she scrap, the farther down she'll keep a'gorn."

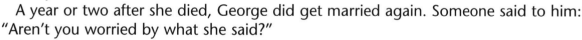

Gert: "They dew say old Fred is a proper gentleman."

Florrie: "Yis – he git up an' open the door for his missus ter bring the coal in!"

After the Event...

MORECAMBE AND WISE AFTER THE EVENT ☞

Ern – *So what do you think of it so far?*

Eric – *Seems like a load of old squit to me.*

Ern – *Just let it wash all over you.*

Eric – *A crab's just bitten my toe.*

Ern – *Which one?*

Eric – *I don't know. All crabs look alike to me.*

Ern – *What did you do during the summer?*

Eric – *I was a lifeguard at Scratby.*

Ern – *What did that entail?*

Eric – *I saved women.*

Ern – *What for?*

Eric – *The winter in Hemsby.*

Ern – *Well, they can't touch you for it.*

Eric – *I've had enough of Cromer. Can we go home?*

Ern – *I've just got to wash my hair.*

Eric – *Then you can hang it out to dry on that bit of wood sticking out over there.*

Ern – *I can't see any piece of wood…*

Eric – *Ah, I told you before – you can't see the groyne!*

Ern – *Is that the best you can do?*

Eric – *It's hard to think with your hat on.*

126